Working and Writing for Change

Working and Writing for Change

Series Editors: Steve Parks and Jessica Pauszek

The Working and Writing for Change series began during the 100th anniversary celebrations of NCTE. It was designed to recognize the collective work of teachers of English, Writing, Composition, and Rhetoric to work within and across diverse identities to ensure the field recognize and respect language, educational, political, and social rights of all students, teachers, and community members. While initially solely focused on the work of NCTE/CCCC Special Interest Groups and Caucuses, the series now includes texts written by individuals in partnership with other communities struggling for social recognition and justice.

Books in the Series

CCCC/NCTE Caucuses
Viva Nuestro Caucus: Rewriting the Forgotten Pages of Our Caucus ed. by Romeo
    García, Iris D. Ruiz, Anita Hernández & María Paz Carvajal Regidor
History of the Black Caucus National Council Teachers
    of English by Marianna White Davis
Listening to Our Elders: Working and Writing for Social Change by Samantha Blackmon,
    Cristina Kirklighter, & Steve Parks
Building a Community, Having a Home: A History of the Conference
    on College Composition and Communication ed. by Jennifer Sano-
    Franchini, Terese Guinsatao Monberg, & K. Hyoejin Yoon

Community Publications

A Parent's POWER by Sylvia P. Simms
The Forever Colony by Victor Villanueva
Visibly (and Invisibly) Muslin on Grounds: Classroom, Culture, and Community
    at the University of Virginia, ed. by Wafa Salah and Fawzia Tahsin
The Lived Experience of Democracy: Criticizing Injustice,
    Building Community, ed. by Kaitlyn Baker, et al.
Steal the Street: The Intersection of Homelessness and Gentrification by Mark Mussman
Literacy and Pedagogy in an Age of Misinformation and Disinformation ed. by
    Tara Lockhart, Brenda Glascott, Chris Warnick, Juli Parrish, & Justin Lewis
Faces of Courage: Ten Years of Building Sanctuary by Harvey Finkle
Equality and Justice: An Engaged Generation, a Troubled World by
    Michael Chehade, Alex Granner, Ahmed Abdelhakim Hachelaf,
    Madhu Napa, Samantha Owens, & Steve Parks
Other People's English: Code-Meshing, Code-Switching, and African
    American Literacy by Vershawn Ashanti Young, Rusty Barrett,
    Y'Shanda Young-Rivera, & Kim Brian Lovejoy
Becoming International: Musings on Studying Abroad
    in America, ed. by Sadie Shorr-Parks
Dreams and Nightmares: I Fled Alone to the United States When I Was
    Fourteen by Liliana Velásquez. ed. and trans. by Mark Lyon
The Weight of My Armor: Creative Nonfiction and Poetry by the Syracuse Veterans'
    Writing Group, ed. by Ivy Kleinbart, Peter McShane, & Eileen Schell
PHD to PhD: How Education Saved My Life by Elaine Richardson

A Parent's POWER

Sylvia P. Simms

Edited by Lori Shorr

Parlor Press
Anderson, South Carolina
www.parlorpress.com

Parlor Press LLC, Anderson, South Carolina, USA

Library of Congress Cataloging-in-Publication Data on File

2 3 4 5

978-1-64317-471-6 (paperback)
978-1-64317-472-3 (PDF)

Working and Writing for Change
An Imprint Series of Parlor Press
Series Editors: Steve Parks and Jessica Pauszek

Interior design by Justin Lewis // justinlewis.me

Parlor Press, LLC is an independent publisher of scholarly and trade titles in print and multimedia formats. This book is available in paper and eBook formats from Parlor Press on the World Wide Web at www.parlorpress.com or through online and brick-and-mortar bookstores. For submission information or to find out about Parlor Press publications, write to Parlor Press, 3015 Brackenberry Drive, Anderson, South Carolina, 29621, or email editor@parlorpress.com.

Contents

Dedication

I dedicate this book to my mother and father, Charles R. Simms and Ella L. Simms, Cole E. Chisholm and Michael S. Hinson R.I.P.

Acknowledgments

I want to acknowledge the many people who have helped me in my life as well as with publishing my memoir. In particular, I want to thank my daughters La'Skeetia Simms and Allegra Simms. My grandchildren Shamiah Simms and A'Sai Simms. My sisters and brother Deborah (Minor), Mary (Dayvaad), Quibila A. (Divine), Charles and Donna Simms.

The work in this book would not have been possible with the following individuals. I send special love to my daughters' fathers, my nieces and nephew, Bikim and every neighbor on the 2700 Block of Opal Street...O'BLOCK,

I want to also thank the members of PARENT POWER old and new, Cecil Parsley, Anna Figueroa, Autumne Hall, Gloria Thomas, Jay Cohen, Angela Lang, and Elizabeth Vargas, Tyson Bryant & family, Dolores Thomas, Darnell Clowney, Summer Weeks, Robert Smith and every brother and sister who live(d) around 19th & Somerset, Woodstock Homes, 24th & Lehigh Ave., the 2700 Ringgold Street.

A Special Thanks To Dr. Lori Shorr

I met Lori when my daughter graduated top of her class, went off to college, and realized she wasn't prepared. Lori and I became not only friends, but sisters. From her placing me on the School Reform Commission, visiting schools together, getting lost and now teaching at TEMPLE...I could have never imagined. Her and her husband Steve asked me if I want to write a book about my life and the things I have accomplished. ME: Who cares about a single mom living in the hood? But because it was Lori, I said yes and was very honored and humbled. I LOVE YOU LORI.

Thank you to the Temple University Students Class of 2023 and 2024.

Remember Families Are YOUR Equal Partners

How This Book Was Created

A Parent's POWER is the result of a series of conversations between Syl
via P. Simms and Lori Shorr which officially began in 2019 but were ini
tiated years before. These interviews were recorded, then transcribed
At this point, Shorr worked with Simms to edit the transcripts into
narrative form as well as clarifying key events or concepts. Through
out, Simms had full editorial control of the content of the manuscript
The goal at every moment was to produce a publication which pre
sented Simms' vision of an equitable education system, but to do so
in her voice that has spoken so powerfully for educational justice in
Philadelphia.

This book is also the result of Simms hard work for parents in the
schools of Philadelphia. In 2009, Simms was "written up" three times
in one day as a result of her advocating for special needs children in
the school where she worked. Despite Simms having a stellar work re
cord over 19 years with the Philadelphia School district, she was re
moved her from her job. With only her position as a bus attendant
which was not full-time, Simms started going to parent workshops
and Title One parent meetings sponsored by the district. There she
met other parents like her and networked them into a new parent or
ganization. They called it PARENT POWER.

✤

Introduction
Lori Shorr

Sylvia and I are friends now. We didn't start out that way. Not that we were enemies either. We just worked from different ends on the same issues – public school reform, educational justice. Over the course of many years, we found ourselves talking to each other more and more. We were having what Sylvia would call a "crucial conversation." Now with *A Parent's POWER*, Sylvia traces the development of her work in sponsoring such conversations among community members, non-profit leaders, city council members, state, and federal representatives.

Back in 2012, I was the Chief Education Officer for the City of Philadelphia during Mayor Michael Nutter's administration – a period also marked by the "Great Recession." One of my responsibilities was to identify and "vet" candidates for the School Reform Commission (SRC), which at that time was the de facto school board for the public schools and consisted of five members jointly appointed by the Pennsylvania Governor and the Philadelphia Mayor. Sylvia and I had already met. My office had sponsored a community presentation on the dropout rate in the city. After the presentation, with her daughter in tow, Sylvia came up asking for the name of a good school for her daughter who was currently out of school. I cannot remember the many little interactions that followed during the year as we shared space being at community meetings, served on the Superintendent's Search committee, and more. When it came time to replace an SRC commissioner, however, I wanted Sylvia. I felt Sylvia had important knowledge about how schools operated on the ground in our lowest income neighborhoods and how families could be a partner in the work of making those schools better. Mayor Nutter agreed.

Now that we are both in different positions, the Mayor and I talk all the time about how little we understood the ramifications of this desire we both had for her to be "at the table," to have her community's values and insights be part of the decision making processes for our schools. Either ignorance or optimism can explain it equally well, but it was one of my decisions.

Sylvia is one of only two commissioners who served out their entire term in the history of the SRC. It was such a grueling, unpaid, high-profile position that few could (or would) stomach it. And during the period Sylvia served the SRC faced its hardest period as a governing body, "the Great Recession." Huge budget deficits started in 2012, such as over $7,000,000 in one year alone. These deficits necessitated massive cuts in personnel and programs which resulted in fights with the unions, contentious community meetings around school closings, and front page stories every week. In fact, for two years in a row, the Mayor announced there was the possibility of schools simply not opening in September. Everyone else on the SRC were lawyers or former government officials. They, at least, had some experience facing the legal and political firestorm of that moment. At the time I asked Sylvia to serve on the SRC, however, she was a bus attendant and a classroom aide for the school district. She had direct experience of how the district was "educating" members of her community — she and her daughters had gone to district schools and her granddaughter was currently a student at a district school. She was not, however, ready for the tumultuous public atmosphere in which her experience would be deployed to improve the schools.

I had promised Sylvia that if she joined the SRC, I would support her. So throughout her tenure, we would meet over lunch to discuss the ever-changing landscape of Philadelphia schools.

We would also take every Thursday to drive around the city in my car — her directing — to make unannounced visits to schools to try to better understand the differences between the *ostensive* vs. *performative* aspect of the district, to use academic language, or to "see what's really happening," to use Sylvia's language. Sometimes we saw amazing things — new after-school programs being launched, students engaged in conversations in classrooms, teachers taking time and care with a child. Sometimes we would see the opposite — run-down buildings with unfriendly staff at the entrance door, front offices locked from the inside so students couldn't enter, teachers in the hallways at their wits end, principals crying in their offices, wondering how they might be better supported. Sylvia took these experiences, blended them with her deep knowledge of the community and educational policy, and used them to advocate for the educational rights of all the city's children.

Even after we both have left our "public roles," we are continuing our conversations. Currently, I am an Associate Professor of Urban Education at Temple University. I have made sure that Sylvia co-teaches one of my classes with me, helping to educate the next generation of teachers. We also work together on community research projects. Sylvia is the Founder/President of *PARENT POWER*, an organization which develops family leaders in low-income neighborhoods in Philadelphia. She also continues to run a summer program for the many children on her block, volunteering her time, her house, her refrigerator – an effort into which she brings her daughters and "the boys on the corner" to serve the free lunches when she can't be there. In fact, a classic "Sylvia moment" is when I am either picking her up or dropping her off at her house, she reaches over and shouts for me to slow down. She then rolls down the car window and yells at a couple of boys sitting on their stoop, "Where's your little brother? Make sure he gets over to my house for lunch today, okay? I didn't see him yesterday. You make sure!" And then without missing a beat, we resume our discussion of how power works on the streets versus "at the table." Spoiler: "It's all game," Sylvia asserts whenever I try to make it more complicated or elaborate. "And I know game" she assures me for the hundredth time.

And she does. Sylvia is what Antonio Gramsci would call an "organic intellectual." For Gramsci, every class has intellectuals that imbue and speak to the values of their original community. The role of organic intellectuals is to explain how their particular fits into the "common sense" of the times, a common sense which keeps certain classes in power and certain classes out of power. As importantly, such intellectuals become permanent persuaders, helping their community understand their true power, helping them organize to change their economic (and educational) status. Which is to say, such organic intellectuals are about the work of changing what counts as "common sense" to redirect resources and assets to those most in need of support. It is about changing systems. And as *A Parent's POWER* illustrates, Sylvia is a master organic intellectual.

Until I met Sylvia, I had liked to fancy myself a radical organic intellectual, having grown up in the steel town of Pittsburgh, having been a first generation college student. I see now that I had actually bought into the meritocracy narrative. Sylvia sees through "game." She sees the contradictions and points them out. She pulls no punches concerning white progressive's rhetoric and the realities of their actions. Witness her story in *A Parent's POWER* where she talks about progressives as trying to give "poor folks windows for their house" when what they need are "floors" — often then acting indignant when the community is not grateful for such "gifts." Or consider her experiences in New Orleans during Hurricane Katrina which highlights how different types of knowledge are always operating. While official instructions were to "go to the Super Dome," her conversation with African-American residents had recommended just the opposite. Her point is white progressives often do not listen or do not "play it straight" with the members of poor communities.

Sylvia listens, however, to her community. For this reason, she possesses the too-often ignored knowledge, subjugated knowledge, that offers true insights. That's Sylvia's stock in trade. And she knows that schools in low-income neighborhoods need parents' "subjugated knowledge" about their children and their community in order to make schools work for their families. Yet time and again, I saw that knowledge dismissed by those in power, whether principals, or district staff, non-profit leaders, or other SRC members. Sylvia tells, here in this book and elsewhere, that she feels she isn't heard. Or to put it another way, people don't listen when she speaks. Or to put it a third way, her insights are not valued, until someone else, from a different subject position says it using more "academic" or "professional" jargon (different words). Then it's an *important* comment, a *keen* insight, maybe even a *game-changing* idea.

But Sylvia was not always dismissed. She made an important impact. Of this, I am certain. But this sense of not being listened to by those in power, more than almost any other topic, is something Sylvia and I discuss almost every time we get a chance. And it is easy to see why it continues to plague her. Why it would plague anybody. Why it does plague everybody who wants to make the world better but is speaking from a place "outside" of the usual trappings of power. It is the question every advocate wonders: did what I say make any difference? I know her insights and critiques of the status quo did influence people's thinking. People with the power to make policy decisions that impact the lives of many Philadelphia students, of which she was one for four years. But she is right to notice, many times in many settings it was pushed aside as either unimportant or the rantings of "an angry Black woman." And that is infuriating. And that is why we teach our master's students in our class how to inspect their own "common sense" assumptions about people and how to detect how privilege gets re-instantiated when we don't do that reflective work.

But I want to underline that this book is not simply about Sylvia's ideas, although it could be since most academics make a living through just ideas. Sylvia's impact can be seen in the work she does every day. I'm always shocked and impressed and humbled when I am at Sylvia's home. There is no boundary between her work and her life. She doesn't leave it at the office. People come to her home and get food from the somehow endless supply she has in the basement or her refrigerator. They come for diapers. They come because their lights are going to be turned off and Sylvia gives them cash — how she does this, I really can't say. Then they come to learn about how they can get their child into a better school or how to talk to a teacher about an issue their child is having in math. And Sylvia will tell them to be sure to register to vote as well. Then, they will come to a workshop she has about how to impact your school's budget. I was at that workshop and on a Friday morning, 24 parents —10 of them men! — showed up in one of the lowest income neighborhoods in Philly to learn about the budget process. They showed up because Sylvia was putting it together and she knows it's important. She has built a cadre of low-income parent leaders by ignoring the boundary of work and homelife, because she lives (and cries and dances) with the people she serves. She is successfully doing the work that literally ever major funder would want to see happen in low-income neighborhoods. She has the template. It's a shame no one funds this type of work anymore. It's the most hopeful, revolutionary work I have seen in my twenty years in urban education. Is it scalable? — a favorite question of every funder. I don't know. But it works. She has the knowledge around this work. But maybe she's right when she says to me all the time, "People in power don't want poor people to be well-educated. It's not in their interest."

Sylvia wanted to do this book so her families, as she calls them, could be better educated about "game," district and schools, and power, etc. I wanted to help her with this book (we did many hours of interviews over the summer of 2019 in my kitchen as the basis for what follows) and make it become a reality because I wanted other people — College of Education students in particular, to be able to learn from her, even when they were not lucky enough to have her as their instructor. So this book is for two audiences. Two groups of people who do not often get to inhabit the same space together. Sylvia and I would often laugh during our Thursday school visit "road trips" at what an unlikely pair we were, driving around in my Prius yelling at each other about which way to turn and often holding back tears — or not—after leaving a school that we didn't feel was kind to the children entrusted to them, or celebrating and singing when the day made us more hopeful. I have learned more about how to be an advocate for social change for our low-income communities from our work together and our unlikely friendship than I ever could have imagined 6 years ago when I asked her to be on the SRC. I hope this book does her work and life and intelligence justice, as she seeks this for her neighborhood and families every day at great personal expense to herself, and she does so not only willingly, but gratefully.

Prologue

A lot of people have come into my life that used me. Okay?

I'm tired of being used, I'm tired of people 'cause a lot of people are not being honest.

A lot of people came to me and said, "Sylvia, you really should do a book." And I was like, I'm not doing a book. I don't trust that it would by *my* book. I don't even read books to be honest. I don't miss it. I'm being honest. So, to write a book, when you came to me, Lori, I didn't know what to do. Maybe I'll start it, not sure I'll finish it, but then . . .

I may cry as I'm telling the story. No, it's okay because I have to cry. If I don't cry, I keep this bottled up in me. And I'm going to tell you something. I'm telling you 'cause I have to in order for me to be sane, okay, because I have really lived a real crazy life. Every day I would wake up, and go, "What the fuck?" I think I'm crying too because that would elevate it. I elevate when I learn something new or if I'm doing something different, and I cry.

Okay.

I went to buy a recorder so I could start to tell my story, keep a record of it, like you suggested. I was asking the lady at the store, "What recorder is this, do you know?" And she was like, "Oh. They really all the same. They all do the same things." Then she said, "Can I ask if you use it for your work? I said, "I'm gonna start my first book about myself and *PARENT POWER*."

She said, "Tell me more about *PARENT POWER*." So, I started talking to her and just telling her about my life, working to get parents the power they deserve in their child's education. She said, "Do you have a card? Because when your book come out, I want to buy it." And I said, "Wow." She wants to hear about my story, my work.

So I think that's why I am a little bit emotional.

Because I'm still here doing the work for families. I'm still building PARENT POWER. My daughters just think I'm crazy and they all say, "Mom, stop it. Just stop it." But I'll say, "I'm doing God's work. I really think that this is what I should be doing. You know, I do. I do. You know, and I still do it cause it's like if I can help one person, one family...

When it's finished, I would like for my families to read this book, and when I say my families, these are the parents and families that I serve — very low income, very impoverished families. These families have so many other challenges that they're dealing with in everyday life that it's kind of hard to be worrying about other things. I think that's why this education system is the way it is today. If I got to worry about going to school or paying my mortgage—or not even a mortgage, my rent—I'm going to worry about paying my rent. I think that's what's happening. So I just want people to understand that they're not out here by themselves. I want their value to be heard across the city.

I also want every educator and every politician to read this book. Everybody who is in a position to make change in policy. I would like this book to be a voice for my families. The people in power need to understand because they're getting paid off the backs of these communities. There's a lot of people out here, and I'm not saying that they're bad people, that's getting paid off the system being the way it is. If the system would get fixed, a lot of people that are getting paid wouldn't be getting paid no more. Then, they would have to find other jobs.

I'm still learning how the world works. I think that's very challenging for me sometimes, being 58 years old. I think that, like a lot of people that live in the world that I live in, they learn things so late in life. It's like we're always playing catch-up. So this is my story of gaining an education in the world, then attempting to change it for the children of my families.

I want this book to speak their concerns.

I want to be one of the voices of the voiceless.

That's one of my favorite sayings.

Chapter 1
I Wasn't Thinking about the Future

I grew up in a house where I had two parents, okay? I had my mother and my father. They were married until they died. My mother and my father were good parents, but they didn't know what they didn't know. And I didn't know that until I became an adult. But they were great parents. They gave us the best. They let us all be who we wanted to be, each and every one of us. They didn't go, "Your sister's doing this thing, we want you to be like your sister."

I have four sisters, one brother. I'm the fourth child. My oldest sister went to college and became a teacher. My next sister dropped out of high school in 12th grade, got a job. At the time, we thought she was very successful, even though she didn't graduate or go to college. Then, there was my next sister, who graduated, went to college, got a couple of Masters' degrees. Then, there's me. Dropped out of high school in the 10th grade, got pregnant. The only reason I went back to high school to get my diploma was because I had a baby. I didn't wanna have a child who saw that their mother didn't have a diploma. So, I went back to school to get my diploma, graduated when I was 21-years old. Then, I had a brother who graduated out of high school. Matter of fact, me and my brother graduated out of high school at the same time. We graduated together. Then, I have a younger sister who graduated and did a little bit of college.

When I was a child, I lived right down the street from the house that I live in now. My mother lived at one end of the block and my grandparents lived at the other end of the block. When I was born, we were the first Blacks on my block. It was all whites on my block when my mother and father moved here. As I got older, other Black families had moved onto the street. When I was in second grade, there may have been like five Black families on the block. As I got older and started working, I did buy me a house, four blocks away. I thought I was really moving somewhere. 'Cause four blocks is a whole different neighborhood. It's a whole different community, you know. I thought I was moving on up. But I look at it now, it's like four blocks. When my grandparents passed away, their house was bigger than my house, so I moved back into their place. Today, all my neighbors are Black.

I went to the neighborhood school until I was in second or third grade. I liked my school. At that time, none of us were getting bussed out because of race. Like my best girlfriend, she got bussed, but she went to another school that was in North Philly, with mostly Black students. My sister, Quibila was in the first round of children getting bussed out of their community for court ordered desegregation. She was in 3rd grade at the time. Then, I was part of the second round. They bussed a lot of us. They had two buses full of children that was picked up at different neighborhoods.

My first school was T.M. Pierce School. I was little, so I don't remember too much of the experience. I knew we used to have race wars because we were going onto other people's turf, white people's turf. It was very interesting because a child being a child don't know stuff unless adults said, "These Black children don't belong here." You understand what I'm saying? Because a child wouldn't go, "Oh, you're Black? Get out my community." It had to be adults telling children something because children wouldn't know. We was just going to school. We made friends across different races. Matter of fact, I used to spend the night at my white friend's house. And to this day, I'm still friends with her.

It wasn't until we got into middle school, when I was at my new school, Woodrow Wilson, that I became aware of the race wars. When we were in elementary school, we got bussed. We came to school on the bus, went right into school, then rode the bus home. It was like we weren't really in the community. So, it wasn't until we got into middle school, seventh grade, when we had to take SEPTA[1] bus to get to school, that we were not on the school bus no more. Now, we were waiting for the public bus in the community.

---

1   SEPTA stands for "Southeastern Pennsylvania Transportation Authority," the public transportation entity that serves the greater Philadelphia region.

So, it wasn't until middle school when we started seeing the prej-
udice, the racism. Now, it might not have been the students in the
school causing the fights. It might've been the older generations
starting the riots. I remember the white people had the bricks and
the stones. The Black brothers had the karate sticks, and they were
knocking the white people with those sticks. We were running to
get on the SEPTA bus, so we could get on the train to get home. We
didn't have the bus attendant to protect us. I didn't know then that
I would later be the lady that was the bus attendant. So, I feel like a
lot of stuff in my life has crossed paths because bus attendants were
the ones that protected us, the students that weren't welcome in
the school. I would later try to do the same.

If something happened to me because of these fights, my
mom was going to kill my sister, Quibila, who also went to Wilson[2]. So Quibila got to drag me along with her to protect me from
the people throwing rocks. Whatever happened to her was going to
happen to me, okay? Quibila is great. She protected me. Kept me
safe. She's A1, okay? Still, I always did things different from her.
She was my big sister. If she went right, I went left. If she went up,
I went down. I didn't want to go where she was going. So when I
got to Wilson, everybody knew Quibila. All the teachers said, "Oh,
she was lovely." "She was just a good girl." "Oh, we love Quibila.
She's great." And I was like, I don't care about you all loving Quibila,
I'm Sylvia. And that probably was the start of me being who I am,
someone who doesn't want to be that goody-goody student. Maybe because people always used to try to compare me to my sister.
So it's like, okay, she's smart, I know she's smart. She save all her
money, she's the good one. So shit, if she's the good one, I guess
I'm the bad one. I think as I grew up, I just was the bad one. I didn't
want to be the one that had straight A's. And if I'm being honest, I
always looked at myself as the underdog.

Quibila and I had some of the same teachers, but because of
who I am, a lot of the teachers didn't like me. I had one teacher who
I think made me not like school. She used to bust on me and say
things that were not nice. I just couldn't believe what she said to

---

me. For instance, this was the period when the Afros was out, the "bushes". I begged my mom to get me an Afro. So, she did. Now, Quibila's Afro was nice. She keeps her locs nice and pretty. My Afro was like my locs now, Rasta. In school, my bush was a mess, but I thought my bush was cool. Then I came to school with my bush the first day. My teacher waited until everybody was sitting in the class and said, "Sylvia, what is wrong with your hair?" I looked at her and I said, "I got a bush." And she said, "It look like you put your finger in an outlet and got electrocuted." This is what this teacher said to me, seventh grade. And we had African American teachers.

I think there are some people who go along to get along and then there are some people who like to bully. And then there's some people who go along to get along *and* like to bully. I have always been like a bully, even when I was young. I always did me. My sister had her clique, but my clique wasn't her clique. My clique was the ones that didn't care. We weren't disrespectful because at the end of the day, we were still children. And my mother and father always instilled respect and integrity, even though we might not agree with somebody else. Still, we were the more militant students, the ones who were going against the grain. The one's saying "You ain't going to tell us nothing."

Now I think I also might have rocked the boat because of my father. My father was a Black man. I mean like a *Black* man. My father had dropped out of high school to go into the military during the Korean War. He saw a lot. It was kill or be killed. I always thought that my mom was the militant one, but in some cases, it was my dad. He was like "Power to the people." Like, "I'm a Black man out here fighting for everything. Nothing is given to you. I got to get out here and work for these white folks all the time." He was working up in the Northeast. He worked in a pipe factory. And he used to always come home and just tell us stories. And, "Yeah, I told that white man. . . 'He probably ain't tell that white man nothing, but I mean, you know, you got to keep the job.'" That was my dad. He had to be a provider, but he was also militant in his thoughts.

After Wilson Middle School, I first went to Parkway Center

City. Here again, I ultimately ended up following my sister, even though I didn't follow her path, if you know what I'm saying. Quibila wanted to go to Gratz where she would be in the Honors program because our sisters had gone there. It was the neighborhood school. Now my mother didn't want me to go to Gratz, so she was like, "You gotta pick another school." I don't know why my mom didn't want me to go to Gratz. I guess she just figured I would probably go to Gratz and mess up. So I said, "Okay, I'm going to go to Parkway." That's when the School District of Philadelphia was just starting the Parkway program, which was a school without walls.

The District was experimenting on students. Okay? And because they didn't have it right, we couldn't have it right. It gave me more flexibility to do things than a brick and mortar school. Because at the brick-and-mortar type of school, I know that at 8:00 in the morning, I had to be at this school. I had to be able to do certain types of work. At Parkway, there was too much freedom. So, a lot of children my age, we just dropped out of school, stopped going to class. I think it was after the first report, my mom was like "You can't stay in this school no more." The only option, though, was Gratz. I didn't want to go to Gratz either, so I started doing the same thing that I was doing at Parkway. I didn't go to school. I cut.

Then boys come into play. This is when I was about 14. Now the only boys I knew was the bad ones. Because at that time, that was my circle that I was hanging with. I wasn't hanging with the B-student boys. I mean, my whole tenth grade year was me pretty much hanging with these bad boys. My mom and dad didn't know because they worked every day, so they didn't know I was hooky-ing. (I didn't call it "playing hooky[3].") And the teachers, they didn't step in. At that time, I thought I was hanging with "the wrong crowd." But when I look back at it now, maybe I was the bad one because I had people that was following me. And I wasn't guiding them in the right direction. I'm like, "Oh, let's go hooky-ing. Let's go cut."

So we were hanging with the boys from the neighborhood.

---

3   Informal term for skipping school

They were older. These were boys that I had a crush on in middle school that now had become high school students. They were the gang boys, the tough boys. Back then, we didn't have drugs, but they used to drink wine. It was different African Americans fighting different African Americans, but it wasn't the guns. It was going in the park and fighting each other. I used to hang out with a gang, *2-0-C Cambria*. That's how I got cool with the boys. I didn't join, though. I just was with them. And since they were with the gang, we became the gang girls. But it wasn't like we was going and fighting other girls. We was just the girlfriends of the boys there.

We had fun though.

I remember it was more my older sisters getting on me about my behavior. It was my older sisters going, "Girl, what is wrong with you?" They were digging in my butt all the time. My next to the oldest sister was the first to drop out. My mom made that sister work with her. That's when they had the factories and all that. But I wasn't thinking about the future. I wasn't. And that's why I can see the future of the children now. Because when you're living day by day by day, you don't see yourself as having a future. You see yourself as today. And if I get past today, I'll deal with tomorrow, tomorrow. And that's what's really going on. And I think that my generation was the first generation to live and think and feel that way. I think this has happened because at some point, society just got into they own self and everyone started doing what was best for them individually.

Remember, this is the 70's. That's a time when *The Jeffersons* came out, "moving on up to the east side." I think we all thought success was possible, we just didn't know how to get there. For instance, when I talk about "the bad boys," a lot of them went to the military. Back then, their only choice was going to the military— whether it was the Army, the Marines, or the Navy—because to escape prison, you had to go into the military. They saw the pathway. And they said, "You know what? We're going into the military." And now a lot of them are successful. Some of them are on drugs because, remember, back then, you had that Crack era, but, as I just said, a lot of them were also successful.

But at that time, when you were middle class or you had Black people that had good jobs, they wanted to be *The Jeffersons*, to move out of their communities to show their success. I had my best girlfriend move. I was like, "Why they moving? We have so much fun on this block." On our block, we all came from good homes. I mean, you know what I'm saying? But a lot of the people that I was hanging with didn't come from two parent households. It may have been a mom or a mom and a boyfriend. So it seemed like the people who was working, who had value and wanted better, moved their families out. The teachers used to live in the neighborhood. The police officers, the people who owned the corner stores, was living in neighborhoods. It was like, all the successful people lived in the neighborhood. Then people that had value or meaningful stuff, they left. So when you leave, what do you leave behind? The people that don't want to have value, to move ahead. In that world, my sister who dropped out of high school became more powerful than my sister who went to college and became a teacher. Because the way we saw it as children, she was giving us everything. "You want a bike?" "Yeah." "Here's your bike." You know? Whereas, my sister, who became a teacher, she was the first one to move out and she moved out into the Northeast[4], the Greater Northeast, where we were bussed. She didn't come around anymore. We looked at her like she was better than us. She was *The Jeffersons*. We were learning to want something else.

My mom always wanted better, always wanted more. We had the best house on the block. We were the first Blacks to have a color TV. We were the first Blacks to have a VCR. So my mom wanted to move us out, but my dad didn't want to move. So we stayed. So we saw the neighborhood change. Because as folks were leaving their homes, there were no longer homeowners coming in. It was renters coming in. Now, there are more renters on my block than homeowners. You have people that come in and don't take pride or value in what is not theirs.

I'm going to be honest, because listen, I call a spade a spade. It seems to me that while you still have some people who live in the

---

4   The Northeast here refers to the Northeast part of Philadelphia

homes they don't own, they don't know the value of the homes they live in and don't value their property. They don't know the value of owning a home. Equity isn't talked about. With equity, I could take my house and get a second mortgage on it. Fix up the house and buy a car. Put my daughter in college. I think what happens in the Black community is "we don't know what we don't know." Nobody has never taught us anything. It's like we always two or three steps behind other folks.

Take Quibila. Quibila went to college, but she chose to stay in the community. Even though she's very successful, she chose to stay. And I asked her "Why did you stay?" You know what she told me? She said, "I want our community to see people that get up and go to work every day. I want them to see people who have nice things. I have a nice house. I have a nice car. I want to let people know that they can have these things too. You don't have to sell drugs and do bad things to have good stuff. You can be a law abiding citizen and have beautiful things too." I didn't know about saving money for beautiful things. Listen, get me money, fuck, it's gone tomorrow. I ain't saving for no rainy day. I might not even be alive to see it's raining. My sister saves, saves, saves, saves, saves, saves. I didn't know about generational wealth until my sister told me about generational wealth. My mother never told me about gener-ational wealth. When my mom passed away, she had money. I got it all. I mean, it wasn't a lot, but you know what I'm saying? When I got it, what did I do? I gave it all away. Now if Quibila would've got it, she would have saved it. I think it's the mindset. She said that's why she stays here. She tries to teach folks a different way.

And I do say folks "don't know what they don't know," be-cause if you knew better, you would do better. I point to the folks that have knowledge that want to keep it for themselves. Folks don't want to share information, knowledge, wealth. I think people have a mentality that thinks, "If I help or bring somebody up that is down, they may knock me off the ladder." It goes back to helping and lifting people up. I look at Philadelphia and I hear this word, "poverty." Poverty, poverty, poverty, poverty. Everybody want to help and reduce and stop poverty. Stop it. You know what you have to do to stop poverty? Help the people that's at their worst and not continue helping the people who are successful. That's why I believe Quibila is the savior of our community. We don't even respect or know it. She comes and talks to me, share her knowledge with me. Since she can't reach the people in our community herself, she tries to reach them through me. Then I try to reach them. That's why I say, we together, but separate. We are trying to help people think about their future.

Chapter 2
I'm Gonna Fight. I'm Serious.

Back in the day, you didn't need a college degree to be a successful citizen. You pretty much didn't need a degree at all. Times change. Now, if you don't have a college degree, it takes you out of getting certain jobs. I was a bus attendant for about seventeen years for the School District of Philadelphia. A bus attendant works with special-needs children. They sit on the bus with the children and help during the trip to and from school. Back then, you didn't need a college degree to be a bus attendant. Now, you have to be highly qualified. You have to pass a certain test. I didn't have to pass a test when I got my job.

Bus attendants have a choice of going inside the school. You can walk in with the children as a one-on-one aide. I was a one-on-one. I was working with one child. But because I had done this job for so long, I didn't only work with my child. I worked for the whole class of special needs students, even though I was a one-on-one. I worked with children who could not speak, children that were emotionally challenged, children who were learning disabled, mentally and physically challenged. I did it all. I was that bus attendant who everybody with a problem would say, "We gotta go get Sylvia to work with the worst, toughest child." I think they knew I loved the children. That it wasn't about me. It was about what could I do to make that child's life better in that day that I had them. And I loved that job. I really loved that job. Working with those children, I felt as though somebody needed me. I loved serving those children, I did.

To be honest, that's what made me become an advocate. It was working with those special needs children and seeing folks doing a disservice to them. For a long time, I was working with a great school that had everything these children required. See, these are children with special needs, but they can function given the proper tools, life skills. They are able to become productive citizens. Then, our school was closed down, which means the children had to go somewhere else. They sent the children to a great school, an excellent school, for the *average* student, but it didn't serve these children with *special* needs. I know what we had at the first school, but we weren't getting these supports at the new school. They gave those children nothing. They put us in a classroom with only chairs and a table. It was wrong. It was just wrong. When I discovered it wasn't serving the children's' needs the way I thought should be the case, I became an advocate.

Of course, I didn't know exactly about the education that they should have gotten or didn't get. I just knew that we were at a great school prior to going to the new school. At the other school, it was nice. I enjoyed the people. I was pretty much able to do whatever I needed to do to serve the children. It wasn't until I got to the new school that barriers were put up for these children. Things that I was able to do at the old school, I wasn't able to do at the new school. Like, we had a schedule at the old school. When the children came in, we had breakfast. We did the brushing of their teeth, the combing of their hair, you know, the life skills to help them be on their way. But at the new school, we didn't have anything but tables and chairs. In my personal opinion, I began to think there were folks at this new school that didn't want that population of children in their school. So, because they didn't want us in the school, they didn't give us the tools we needed to serve the children.

So, I began fighting for those children and their right to attend a school that met their needs. I went to the principal on several occasions and told her that we don't have the tools and resources that we needed to serve the children. She was putting barriers up to us serving the children. Like I said, she put us in a room that didn't have a sink so we couldn't brush the children's teeth. She also wouldn't let us go downstairs in the bathroom to use those sinks. She wouldn't let us put our refrigerator in our classroom where we can give our children snacks. It was all kinds of barriers that this principal was putting up to stop us from serving the children.

Now, because I had seniority, I could have gone to other places, but this teacher had begged me to go with her to the new school. She said, "Sylvia, please come. We need you." She knew this principal wasn't going to support her. She begged me. She figured if I come, I have the big mouth, I'm gonna fight. I'm serious. So I rolled with her, I went, and I got caught up in this foolishness. At first, me and my teacher were fighting together, but I think they started messing with my teacher. She was like "Sylvia, I'm not fighting this fight anymore." So after a point, the teacher stayed out, but I continued to fight because I'm not afraid.

At that point, the principal and folks started bothering me. For instance, I got written up three times in one day, which is unheard of. The first write-up stated, "It has been brought to my attention that you have not been escorting a student who you provide one-on-one service off the bus into the school. You are directed to perform all duties assigned to you, and if you have any questions..." blah, blah, blah. So this was my comeback: I said I wanted the date and time, prove what happened. To me, it's all hearsay. It's also not clear that it was my responsibility. Prior to this moment, they always came and got him off the bus.

My second write-up: "On March the 20th and the 21st, I observed you sleeping in Room 101. Sleeping during scheduled work hours is prohibited. You are directed to stop sleeping during scheduled work hours in any part of the building. Failure to follow these directions would result in further disciplinary actions, which may include suspension and unsatisfactory rating, and/or termination." Okay. Yes, I sleep. But to go to work, I get up at three o'clock to catch the SEPTA bus so I can be there in the morning to get to the child's house, which was in the far Northeast, Bensalem. It took about an hour and a half to get there. I usually get to his house about 5:30 – 6:00 a.m. Then, we would get to school between 8:30, 9:00 in the morning. My lunch was from 2:00 to 2:45 and I'm on my lunch break before I get back on the bus. So what if I sleep?

Finally — and here I think her real motivation become clear — she wrote: "It has been brought to my attention that you have been challenged in the duties and responsibility of various school district employees assigned at this work location. Your actions have subverted the climate in the classroom and negatively impacted the students in your care. Effective immediately, you are directed to refrain from challenging the duties and responsibility of other school district employees assigned to Greenberg Elementary School. Failure to follow these directives will result in disciplinary action on it." So I asked, "What specific actions should I refrain from? What does that mean? Who did I challenge? When? What duties? What date? What?" She didn't say.

I think she was referring to a time I was telling her about the lack of service we were giving to the children in the classroom. I had said to her, "You left us in the classroom with nothing but table and chairs. We had nothing to work with. All our stuff was locked up in the basement that we couldn't get to, to help our children be successful students." I was only saying this because the teacher was saying, "Sylvia, you meet with her." Maybe because I'm Black and the principal is Black. The teacher was white and a new teacher. Remember the teacher asked me to come with her, to advocate for the children. So me being me, I stand up for the children. I go talk to her. That's when the principal told me, "I don't want these kids in my school." Then she wrote me up three times, really, in one day.

So she gave these letters to me all at once. Each in their own envelope. She gave them to me on a Friday and told me, "Don't come back to the school." My first thought is you can't do that. I've got to have union representation. You can't even give this to me without talking to my union. I knew that because I had read the contract. But the union didn't end up supporting me. They wound up saying, "Sylvia, don't go back into the school." But see, what they didn't realize is when I didn't go back to their school, they cut my money. I was getting paid for a whole day because I was going inside the school, working with the one-on-one. The school said, "We're going to make you Bus Attendant auxiliary." Auxiliary means we just ride the bus. You don't go into the classroom. You don't do nothing. Just ride the bus. Come home. That whole day break is yours, and in the afternoon, you get back on the bus.

They thought they had beat me. But though I was making less money, it was actually great for me. I figured, y'all gave me all this free time now, so I just took the free time and learned how to become an advocate for *all* students, not just those with special needs. What I did was I started going to the Philadelphia School District offices, also called "440."[5] I went to all the workshops and seminars being offered. I just got off the school bus and jumped on the subway straight down to the district, where I messed with people all day. I was a pain in their butt. Then I'd go back to the school, do my work as an auxiliary, then back home. I became concerned about not just one school, but all the schools that were failing students.

And, really, that's how *PARENT POWER* started.

---

5   The School District of Philadelphia offices are referred to as "440" because of their address, at 440 N Broad Street.

Chapter 3
She Used to Tell Us, "I'm going to lose
my job doing my job."

When I started going to the district every day, Quibila was the parent and family engagement person. I was just constantly ragging her, just telling her how the school district is bad and how they treat people. Just every day saying, "Oh the school district is no good 'cause they did me wrong." She said, "Why won't you get involved?" I'm like, "I am involved." You know, I'm doing this, I'm doing that. She said, "No, being involved means more than that. Try coming to my workshops." Since I was now a Bus Attendant Auxiliary, I had time to go to one of her workshops on *No Child Left Behind*.[1] I remember it like it was yesterday. I learned so much in that two hours that I didn't know the whole 17 years that I was working for the School District of Philadelphia. I was in awe. It was like, "Wow. I'm sitting up here working for the school district for all these years and never knew about *No Child Left Behind*." Never knew what it was. Didn't know about the types of schools we had. I didn't know none of that stuff. That's when I realized there's a lot of stuff out here that my people don't even know about.

I started just going to all the District's workshops and trainings. Just going to all the parent meetings. Still not liking the district, but now learning from it. I also became involved with the *Parent Leadership Academy*[2] and going to their workshops. I'm going to tell you, *Parent Leadership Academy* and the *Family Leadership Institute*,[3] those were the best parent-run organizations. They built all the parent community leaders in Philadelphia. Now, when you look back, a lot of them got jobs in Philadelphia's Department of Human Services. They think they are able to continue to advocate. But once you become an employee, the system is able to hush you up because you gotta take care of family. You don't want to lose your job. So you become less powerful, even though you might think you have gained power by being accepted into the system.

It wasn't until we got a new Superintendent, Dr. Arlene Ackerman[4], that I knew I was powerful enough to advocate without needing to be part of the District. When she first arrived in the District, I would go up to her every time we were in the same place and say the same thing: "How ya doing? My names is Sylvia Simms. I got written up three times in one day and kicked out of my school." "How ya doin? My name is Sylvia Simms. I got written up three times in one day and kicked out of my school." "How ya doin? My name is Sylvia Simms. I got written up three times in one day and kicked out of my school." So every time I would see this woman, that's what I would say to her.

I was telling her that because for months, everybody in the school district knew what was happening to me, but nobody did nothing. For me, this was like, "Hey, we got a new Superintendent. Maybe she can help me." So that's why every time I would see her, I would say that. I said it about 10 times. Then, one time that we were at this parent workshop, she said, "Miss, you say the same things to me all the time. What is it that you're saying?" So, I said it again. She said, "Come up to my office." I went up to her office and we talked. We became very good friends. She listened to me. She listened to the families. Things that I knew that were needed to help the families, she gave us. So that was when I knew that, as a parent, I had the power to change minds, to change how money was being spent. That is when I started *PARENT POWER*.

Here's how it started. *Parent Leadership Academy* had funding from the William Penn Foundation to do parent engagement work when I first came around. Soon after I talked to Dr. Ackerman, I was actually on my way to *the National Coalition of ESEA Title 1 Parents Conference[5]* in Virginia, which was the first conference I ever attended. And, my God, I tell you these were some powerful women. They knew that *Title 1* stuff. I was just amazed. That's how I heard about the term *PARENT POWER*. A presenter was talking about *Title 1*. She did all this talking about how families need to be involved. At the beginning, at the top of the first presentation slide was "PARENT POWER." But at the end, on the last slide, it had, "PARENT POWER: What will you do with yours?" I said, "Oh my God, can I take this to Philadelphia?" She said, "Yes, you can take it. You can do it." Then, I went back to Dr. Ackerman. I said I want to do something differently. I want to start my own parent organization. I want you to help and support it. I guess she just saw something in me. I don't know what she saw in me, I don't know if she saw my passion. But she was always like, "You are so smart, you can be anything you want to be." So after I told her my idea, she said, "Start your own parent organization." That's what I did.

When I started *PARENT POWER*, it was at the time when I was also getting really heavily involved in my union. I had to make a conscious choice: Do I want to do *PARENT POWER* and advocate for families or do I want to become the leader of all the bus attendants in Philadelphia? This is when I didn't even know I was an advocate. I mean, I was advocating for myself about my firing. But, being a bus attendant, who is going to listen, who is going to believe me? It had even gotten to a point where people were saying things like, "Sylvia, go in the corner and shut up. Nobody's listening to you." I thought they were going to help because that's their job. I paid union dues. I thought the union was supposed to protect people. This didn't seem to be the case. I was learning that by myself, I didn't have much power. That the system didn't want to listen to me. I thought about the parents who were not being listened to by the district. And I thought, since *PARENT POWER* was mine, I felt as though I could control it. I could build something that would listen to these parents and help protect their children. I could do it differently than the district and the union. So, I chose to build the parent organization.

Remember now, Quibila was the parent person in the district. She had been there since the previous Superintendent, Paul Valles[6]. But when Valles was there, she couldn't do what she came to do. It wasn't a priority for him. We also had the *Home and School Association,* the parent organization for the district. It was Quibila's job to work with all parent organizations and she did that. For some reason, members of the *Home and School Association* felt they deserved more than other parent organizations and Quibila treats everyone equally. Still.... And this is no disrespect to people, but when you have Black people that are just "yes men" and "yes women," you are just a "yes man" for a white face. If the leader says, "This is what we're doing," you're going to do it or you're going to have controversy with the leader. He's going to kick you off, because you're not agreeing to what he wants. You have people that go along to get along. They stay in position longer. So, I thought we needed an organization like *PARENT POWER,* something independent that supported poor parents fighting for their children's education.

Quibila always used to say, "I'm going to lose my job doing my job." And I do have to give a lot of homage to Quibila because she grew me to help others. Do you understand what I'm saying? She used to say, "When you go to the school as one angry parent, they see you as one angry parent. But if you go to the school with five angry parents, they can't see you all as five angry people because you're all saying and fighting about the same issue. Now, they have to listen to you." Then she said, "Let me tell you what to do, how to do it and how to be an organizer." I'd go "Wow, that's what you do, huh?"

Quibila did actually lose her job. I think she got laid off because she was educating low-income families to turn around and go against things that we had always accepted. That's why a lot of districts don't do parent education. Because if you start educating folks, they will have knowledge to go against you. You *gave* parents the tools to go against you. That's what Quibila knew. That's what she taught us. So with *PARENT POWER,* when parents had issues, I'd go, "Wait a minute, let me get a couple more of my parents and we're going to come with you." That's what we did at first and a lot of times, it helped. Sometimes they listened, sometimes they respected us. But at each moment, we were learning together.

We were building PARENT POWER.

Chapter 4
"What Will You Do with Yours"

When I first came to School District workshops and meet-ings, I was a parent that didn't know, didn't care. And because I stayed, I started wanting more education and information. Then I became a parent leader. Once you become a parent leader, there has to be somebody that sees something in you and puts you somewhere, like a job at a non-profit. But somebody's got to see something in you to do that. It's rarely parent leaders who do it by themselves. You have to know somebody in a higher level to pull you up and to not be afraid to help you. You understand what I'm saying? I wanted *PARENT POWER* to be that organiza-tion that pulled parents up and saw their potential.

I was going to these *Title 1* workshops and learning so much. We learned about Lyndon B. Johnson's *War on Poverty*[7]. All of this was new to me. When the *War on Poverty* began in 1965, I was five years old, I was just beginning kindergarten. I began to realize that all of this stuff that was going on in my advocate life was really connected to my personal life. Do you understand what I'm saying? I didn't know all this stuff until reading and picking it apart, I was digging deep. I mean, it was just good, you know? I was also just learning all this stuff about the *Elementary, Secondary Education Act*[8]. I was learning how new presidents al-ways change the names of education programs to highlight what they were now doing.

When I started going to the workshops, George W. Bush had *No Child Left Behind*[9]. So what I started doing is reading the policies of the program. I learned that the district was supposed to give you a piece of paper that tells if your school is failing and what's supposed to happen in response. In the first year, the school should get a warning. The second year, if your school was still failing, there had to be a corrective action. If your school fails the third year, there are more things that happen. Then, I think after five years, if your school has been failing and not making an *Annual Yearly Progress*, *No Child Left Behind* mandates that the principal gets removed and that the school is turned over to new leadership.

So, I'm sitting up reading these policies. Remember, Dr. Ackerman is the Superintendent, who I like and admire. But I'm like, "Wait in a minute. These things are supposed to happen, but they are not happening." I started telling the parents. I'd say, "This is law. These are the policies. These are the things that should be happening that's not happening." I started teaching other parents what I was learning about laws, policies, and what's supposed to go on in their schools. Remember, we all had children or grandchildren or nieces and nephews in failing schools, okay? This was when I started having my *PARENT POWER* meetings. So, we're having our meetings. We're coming together.

Then what I started doing was going to the District's meetings. I was going to District meetings believing I'm going to get these parents on my side and into *PARENT POWER*. I was going to *Title 1* District meetings. I was going to every meeting the District had. For instance, Dr. Ackerman—who, God bless her, always gave us what we asked for—began to have Superintendent meetings. She would have thousands of parents coming. I used to just sit and listen to all of the angry parents. After an angry parent got up and said what they had to say, I would go to them and say, "Hi. How are you doing? My name is Sylvia Simms. Can we talk to you about what's going on in your school?" They're already angry. They're upset. They're hurt. Then I would ask them to join *PARENT POWER*.

PARENT POWER is different from other organizations because of the families involved. I live their life. I go through the same tribulations that they go through. It's not like I'm coming from a land that I don't know trying to help these people. I live this day in and day out. There's a lot of families out here that are struggling more than I am, that have different issues, living in different types and kinds of poverty that I'm not. I respect the families, which too often non-profit or educational organizations do not. Of course, they say they respect them. But, really, it's just their job. I mean, working with our population is helping their own families, making sure their own bills are getting paid. You understand what I'm saying?

I'm not saying that they don't care, but if you never lived in poverty, if you never had anything cut off in your house, then that's a whole other world you don't understand. For me, I don't judge people. My thing is, I talk to you. I ask, "How can I help you?" "How can I assist you?" And if you don't want it, fine. But if you're around me tomorrow, I'm coming back, "Hey how can I help you?" "How can I assist you? You need anything?" I'm not going to know that you need something and turn my head away. I think that the families that I do serve, and I do touch, they know that I'm genuine. That's why they love me and I love them. I'm coming out of a space of love. I'm not coming from a space where this is my job. I'm coming out of a space of this is my passion. I want to see you better yourself, so you can make sure your child is not living in the same conditions that you are. I built *PARENT POWER* to be a place that respects you, your knowledge, and helps you become a powerful advocate for your child — to be that support that pulls you up.

Take a typical day for me. I get two, three, four, five, sometimes six phone calls. I'll get phone calls from families who are crying, upset, disenfranchised because they don't know what to do to stop something from happening to their child in school. They don't know what to do about their electric, gas, or water bill that they can't pay. And sometimes, I can help them, because like I said, I am the families that I serve.

Regardless, I'm always listening. Do you understand what I'm saying? I listen. Then, I try to seek out the help that I think they need. I always give them my number. And I don't even ask. I put my number out there so much that a friend told a friend who told a friend to call me. That's how I think people get connected. It's by word of mouth. "Oh, well yeah, I know Sylvia. Sylvia has this organization called *PARENT POWER*. She's a parent advocate." So people that I know, or know me through a friend, just give people my number.

When parents join *PARENT POWER*, I believe, first, you got to give them love. You have to listen. You just can't say, "Oh, we're having a problem and now we're going to fight." They want somebody to listen to them too. So, I was the listening ear to my families. We listened, offered respect, and assisted them. Like I said, we have a lot of challenges. But when we became a group, we walked together as one. We all had our *PARENT POWER* shirts on. We were there supporting each other in our children's school. Sometimes we didn't even know what we were doing when we went to a school. I'm a community organizer but I didn't ever go to some community organizer school. I just did it because there was a need. I just did it because I wanted to help people. And I think I'm the best community organizer without even knowing how to be a community organizer. Because I'm quite sure there are things that you're supposed to do to be a community organizer, like listen, support, respect. I made sure *PARENT POWER* did that. And that's one way that we grew larger.

Gradually, other people began to hear about *PARENT POWER*. Beyond going to meetings, we really seemed to get on people's map through *Facebook*. I am old school. I am very, very old school. I didn't get on the internet until very late in life because I was afraid of it. That's how old school I am. My youngest daughter and her friends, they're just social media people. I was just starting *PARENT POWER*, and my daughter said, "Mom, if you really want to blow *PARENT POWER* up and let people know what it is, you need to start a *Facebook* page." I was like, "I'm not starting no *Facebook* page." But then I had a girlfriend that actually made posts for me. She showed me how to get on *Facebook*, how to use it to promote *PARENT POWER*. And as I met politicians, I took pictures with them while wearing my *PARENT POWER* t-shirt. That made people think that I was important. I was connected. That helped *PARENT POWER* become known to the public.

But with that, I need to say that those type of important people don't impress me. What impresses me is people doing the work. I love people that really are on the ground, actually doing the work that a lot of people don't notice. People that's really out here helping people that don't know what they don't know. Don't know how to navigate things. Real grassroots organizations are so grassroots that they're under the dirt. There's a lot of us out there that's doing the work, but we're the ones that don't get noticed. We're the ones that don't get recognized. We don't do the work to get noticed, to get recognized, but we are the ones that are dealing with people on personal levels every day.

With all of this happening, I think it wasn't until my granddaughter was living with me that I began to understand what *PARENT POWER* needed to do to begin to help parents change schools, what it needed to make sure their children would get a real education. I was on my granddaughter's CASTOR Form which meant if anything happened to her, I would be contacted if the parents were not available. But it's actually bigger than that specific issue. It's not just an identification form. It's a form that means this person has the educational experience, or whatever, to be in this child's life. I'd made sure my name was on my granddaughter's form, so I could be involved, so that the school district could not say, "You can't be involved."

At the time, I was sitting on a State Advisory Council[10] serving families. My voice always rings out, because I'm a fighter. I'm always that person that will stand up and speak out for the people. So, I was sitting on this Council that was ran by the Pennsylvania Department of Education. I was an advocate because people at the State don't like Philadelphia. So now you've got a parent up there who knows her stuff, talks her stuff, talking her stuff to the folks in Harrisburg. Even though I might not have a degree, I'm very knowledgeable. I loved being on the Council because I was also continuing to learn so much information. I was meeting parents from across the state. I was organizing them. It wasn't only me that was trying to organize the parents across the state. It was a lot of people.

But I think that when you go against the grain, there are folks that became afraid of you because they cannot control you. I see that wherever I go. And I know that scares a lot of people. So, they got me off the board. They removed me. They said, "You don't have children in a School District of Philadelphia." And I'm like, "Yes, I do, I have my granddaughter. I'm on her CASTOR Form." They wanted me to show proof. Well, when I got the form, my name had been removed. Somebody in 440, the School District Office, took my name off of that form. So I went to the school. I went to the regional office. I went to the *Title 1* office because, you remember, everything I was doing was under the *Title 1* office. And *Title 1* is supposed to help low income families, that's the purpose of *Title 1*. The *Title 1* office controlled everything around family and community engagement.

I was going through them and nobody did nothing — from the top person to the parent organizers. Nobody. They were all like "You're off." And I think it was because the State Department of Education was like, "We don't want her." The School District of Philadelphia aren't going to go against the State. It just shows you how it works when people don't have balls, when people are afraid to push back. This is why we get what we get. Because it could only take one person to say, "Why are you doing it to Sylvia? You know Sylvia is fighting for the children in Philadelphia. She's a great advocate. Why don't you all want her to be here?" This is what people in power do, they just shun you. Which to me showed the importance of an organization such as *PARENT POWER*, for an organization that kept the needs of parents and students first.

That belief was how some of our first programs started. At

first, *PARENT POWER* was doing part of its programmatic work as the *Positive Peer Program under the EARTHS*. We received a small grant from the *Boys Club of Philadelphia*. And you know what, I'm going to tell you something. When poor people get funded, it may be little bit of money, but we make it work because when you do it with nothing and somebody gives you something, you feel as though you're rich. So what we did is we grabbed all of my daughter's friends and we were like, "Listen, this is what you all are going to do. You all are going to tutor these children at Peirce Elementary." And that's what we did. The goal was to get her back on track and help the children at Peirce. We did it in the basement of my house. It was when Shirley Kitchen[11] first became a senator and she even came to speak to the children.

Then we got the *Community Innovation Zone Grant*[12] for *PARENT POWER*, as an organization. Drexel University was the only other group in Philadelphia that got it. *PARENT POWER* and Drexel. We did a great job with that three year grant. I think we got $74,000. We were able to pay people who before were volunteering their time. We were also able to build Family Engagement Centers at Peirce and Dobbins[6], for instance. Our goal for these centers was to provide a space where families can feel comfortable to talk, feel respected. We'd also help them with daily needs. We would give them access to a computer. We would have a diaper bank there. We'd have a food bank. We'd have a clothing bank. We have books. We have supplies. It was all partnered with other bigger organizations. It's was like a one stop shop. If you don't have what you need, we'll help you find it.

I also learned a hard lesson about doing work in the schools through these Centers. We had prepared to provide resources for the teachers, too. They say teachers don't have a lot of material. So we had all educational games. We had everything. But they didn't even come in there and see. They didn't come. So, I said, when the teachers come back to school after this summer, I'm going to go to their professional development meetings. I wanted to say, "This Family Engagement Center's been here for

---

6   Murrell Dobbins Career & Technical Education High School, also known as Murrell Dobbins Vocational High School, in North Philadelphia.

almost four years." When we first opened it, what I wanted to see in the Center was a partnership with the principal, the school, and the community. (When I say, "the community," I mean the families.) But I think what happened is there was a lot of staff that got jealous. See our room had the air conditioning. It was a beautiful room. It had been repainted. But my thing is, "Okay. We've got this room. Now let's work with a next room." But people won't get out of their own way. It's like people don't want to collaborate. But I told them, it's everybody's room. I don't think it was portrayed by the principal like that. I had talked to different teachers and said, "Come on in." And even though I said that they still wouldn't come in.

I think everybody is trying, but it's a hard job to be in education. It's hard to be a parent. It's hard to be a community partner. It's hard to be a teacher. It's hard to be in leadership. And because nobody talks to each other, communication becomes key. If people would communicate, there's a lot of barriers that can be broken. We tried to have these critical conversations in the *Family Engagement Centers* with the community. For instance, once we had a workshop on how school budgets work. We had 25 parents there and 10 of them were African-American men, which was rare for such events. And there was another one that I thought was the best. That was when I got all the system superintendents that worked in my neighborhood to come to a meeting. See we have the Turnaround schools, Charter schools, Traditional Public schools, Mastery schools, KIPP schools, Catholic schools in my neighborhood[13]. What I did was I got all those leaders to come to the *Family Engagement Center* to have a conversation. Because at the end of the day, my thing is, we all serve children who live in our community. We're all serving the same population. That's when I got kicked out of Dobbins. I believe that was this conversation. I was really trying to help families come together at the grassroots level with charters and public. It was great. But I really believe the district got scared when I did that because it was getting all the systems to work together, not making the District the most important organization but one amongst many.

36

Today, we only have a *Family Engagement Center* in one school. More still could exist, but the leadership of those other schools didn't want them. And it's sad because we are doing nothing with the Center at Peirce. We still have a room. We still call it a *Family Engagement Center*, but it could be better. We don't really have anyone to staff it. When we had the grant, we had staff to keep it open every day, all day. That money is gone. So now, we just come in when we can. My daughter works at Peirce, so before she goes to work, she volunteers in the center. Then it's open again when she gets off of work. I'm not working now, so I'm over there more, just trying to help the families with their needs. Neither of us gets paid.

But to be honest, I'd rather just have my own space outside the school. What I'm finding out is people in my neighborhood, they don't feel welcome in the school. So things that we are doing in the school, a lot of families are not coming because they had a bad experience in that school when they were children. Also, when it's in the school, people know people's business. They may need some diapers or may need some food or may need some milk. And when you come into the room, you don't know what other people are thinking. But I tell them, "Don't worry what other people think about you." That's why I tell them, "Listen. Everybody's had ill wills. Everybody has challenges. You may not think they do, but everybody is going through something, or has been through something. Even the wealthy." Just because you've got money and have everything, that doesn't mean you are happy. You might have nobody who loves you. You may have all of the money in the world, but if you ain't got love ... You know? I just try to uplift people and give them love. If I could get our own space, then I could really serve the families, because that's a space where they will be comfortable like when they are coming into my house. And then, we could have the real conversations that need to happen to help the children. Because my thing is, why can't we?

I'm beginning to think that no one really wants those conversations to occur. Here's an example. It's a day I'll never forget. Dr. Ackerman had left the District. It was the day now Superintendent Hite came for his job interview. I was on the Search Committee and was asked to take Dr. Hite[14] to all these schools and all these meetings. I got up like 5:00 a.m. that morning to meet Dr. Hite. We rode around all day going to all the schools. That evening, there was a final meeting with the community, but there was also a *Title 1 Parent Advisory Council*[15] meeting as well. So, I said, "Well, I'm going to just dip into the that *Title 1* meeting, then I'm gonna leave to go up with Dr. Hite to his meeting." It was me and about seven of our *PARENT POWER* members.

But the parent, family, and community engagement people, people who are supposed to drop the barriers so the community could be involved, locked us out. I mean they actually locked the door and would not let us in. It was an open meeting, but the District didn't want us there. *PARENT POWER* knew their *Title 1* shit. We knew our stuff. The district wanted their own parents, parents who would just sign off on whatever the district wanted to do. Whereas we would've said, "Oh no, no. We ain't going for that." It would have been a conflict. "We ain't just sign off on something because y'all say, cause we know better."

Now remember, I had spent all day with possibly the new Superintendent. So, when they didn't let us in, I was done. I swear when I tell you, I was done. I was like, "That was the last door that the district could shut on me." I was on my way to the *Philadelphia Inquirer*, cause the newspaper's building was right down the street. I'm like, I'm on my way. "Come on y'all. We going to the *Inquirer*." I don't care. I'm crying cause, "They wouldn't let us in the room." I'm crying and I'm walking down to the paper, cussing. Then Pedro Ramos[16] comes out now. Pedro was the chair of the School Reform Commission[17] at the time.

He's like, "Sylvia, what's going on?" I was like, "Fuck you." I said, "I'm going." He said, "Sylvia I'm telling you. Get into this office." I don't know what made me go into his office. I guess in my heart, I didn't want to go against the District cause, I do like the District. I try to work with them, even though sometimes you can't work with them. So, I'm in his office, I'm crying and my parents are with me. He said, "What's going on?" I said, "They locked us out the meeting." Then someone from the SRC office came in as well. She found out what was happening. She went into the *Title 1* meeting and said, "I'm making the executive decision. You let these parents in this room." But I was like, "If you treat me like this, why you think I want to be in here?" So I didn't go, but I told a couple of my parents, "Y'all go get in there so we can know what was going on."

So then I went up to the meeting with Dr. Hite. I wasn't going to speak, but I spoke and told how people were treating families. How this is the bullshit that goes on in the school district filled with people locking doors, locking you out of parent meetings. This happens to parents all the time. I mean this, it's nothing that's new for parents. That's what started *PARENT POWER*.

I'm not even gonna make it about race because I also think it happens to wealthy parents that don't go along with the status quo. I think that if you're not going along with the system, whether you rich or poor, it happens, but it happens mostly to poor people. Rich people have money. They can say, "No you ain't doing nothing cause I'm taking my money out of the school." But I hear stories of how sometimes, poor parents are treated poorly... I can't believe it.

So, after being taken off the State Advisory Council and a couple of days after being locked out of the school district *Title 1* Meeting, after starting *PARENT POWER* as an independent advocacy group, I was asked to be one of the Commissioners on the Philadelphia School Reform Commission.

I was offered power. Now what would I do with mine?

Image 1. The Women of Sylvia P. Simms' Family.

Image 2. Sylvia P. Simms, LaSkeetia Simms, Shamiah Simms, Allegra Simms and John K. Austin on O'Block

Image 3. Darnell Clowney, La'Skeetia Simms, Allegra Simms, and Sylvia P. Simms.

Image 4. The Men of Syliva P. Simms Family.

Image 5. Syliva P. Simms and Michael Hinson.

Image 6. PARENT POWER in Park.

Image 7. Allegra Simms, Florence Arthur, Ryan Bland, Angie High-
tower, and Sylvia P. Simms on O'Block.

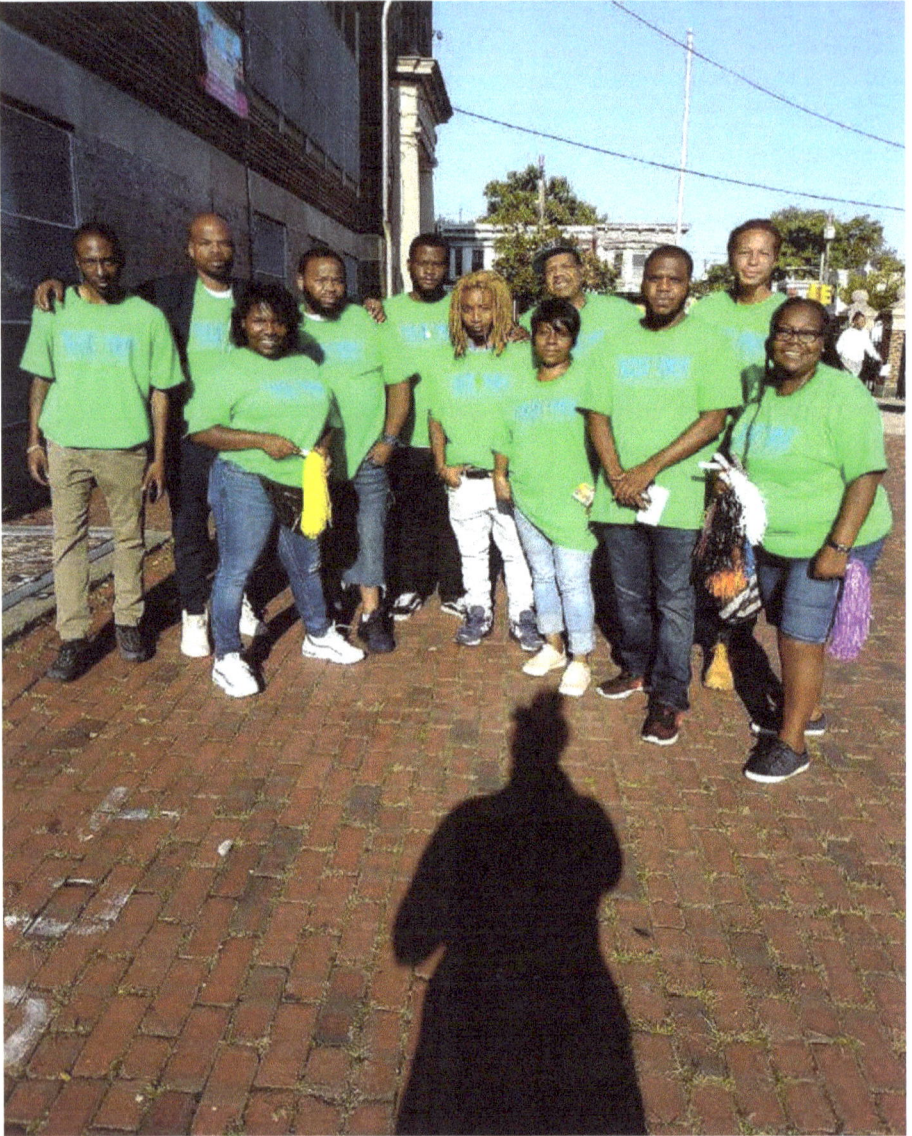

Image 8. PARENT POWER at T.M. Peirce first day of school.

Image 9. PARENT POWER Shirts.

Image 10. Quibila A. Divine, Sylvia P. Simms, Charles R. Simms (Dad), Mary Simms (Dayvaad).

Image 11. Opening of the Family Engagement Center at Dobbins High School (now closed) with members of PARENT POWER.

Image 12. PARENT POWER with Mayor Michael Nutter.

Image 13. PARENT POWER with Dr. Ackerman First Home Visit.

11/16/2009

Image 14. Sylvia P. Simms' parents, Charles R. Simms and E. Lucille Simms.

Image 15. PARENT POWER Shirt.

Image 16. PARENT POWER member with Lisa Nutter.

Image 17. Sylvia P. Simms and Lori Shorr on Vacation.

Image 18. Mayor Michael Nutter swearing in Sylvia P. Simms as School Reform Commissioner, with La'Skeetia Simms in attendance.

Image 19. The Simms family with Deborah Minor, Donna Simms, Charles R. Simms III, Kellen Simms, Kalina Simms, Irene Anthony.

Image 20. Quibila A. Divine and Syvia P. Simms.

Chapter 5
"Until y'all fix the schools in my community, I'm not going anywhere. I'm not."

I was very, very surprised to be asked to be on the School Reform Commission, especially because at the time I was going through stuff with the district — being treated unfairly, getting taken off of the State Advisory Council. Why did I do it? I did it because I wanted to get them back. That was my first thought. I'm going to be on the Commission that can get that District and get them people for not serving the children. Hold them accountable. Make sure they're doing right by families. I was always coming from a family perspective of what we can do to help the families to help their children. I saw things as a system. I want to speak for my parents. To make change. Now I served with a whole lot of commissioners and everybody was unique. Everybody who I served with brought something unique to the table. But they didn't listen to me the way they listened to the other commissioners. I was always the parent speaking for poor parents. I felt they never listened to me.

In fact, I cried a lot. I did. I cried a lot in those meetings because they just weren't listening. You know when somebody's not listening to you. You can't punch them in the mouth, which I wanted to do a lot of times. So, I just ran out the room or gave them the finger. I did, I gave them the finger a lot because it was like "Why am I here?" And I lost a lot of people who I thought were my friends when I became a commissioner. I think a lot of them looked at me like "How the hell is she a commissioner?" Like, "Why her? Why not me? I'm better. I'm smarter. I'm richer." I honestly think even the politicians were like, "Who the fuck is Sylvia?" I was a poor Black parent. And it wasn't like I had people that asked, "Sylvia, you okay? Are you all right?" No one ever grabbed my hands and said, "This is what you should know."

I didn't have anybody. I had my family. I had my parents. But that was it. That was it. Lot of times I thought about leaving. But I said to myself, that if I leave, who are they going to put in my place? If I leave were they going to get another Sylvia Simms? Somebody who really stands up for the poor families and speaks up? See it's one thing being a part of something, but if you just are part of something to be that person, at the table, what's the point? If you are not speaking up, why be at the table? So I tried to be the voice for the voiceless. So that's why I stayed the whole four-year term. I tried to be the voice for those other parents who were not being listened to by people in power.

All I wanted to do on the School Reform Commission was to put policies in place that would help families. I thought, if I can get these several key things done, then we are going to be okay. And I got 'em done. I helped to establish a policy for *School Advisory Councils*[18] that gave parents more power in the schools. I help to expand who counted as a parent for children. Remember, before, the District saw parents and not families. But a lot of poor people, a lot of poor children, don't have parents. They may have a grandma raise 'em. I mean, my granddaughter has a mother and a father who are very active in their life, but at the time they were working nine to five. I had free time because they kicked me out of the school where I had been working. Now, I've got nothing but time. So, my time is going to be spent making sure my granddaughter is successful in school and in life. Like why put up barriers to block this grandma to be involved in their grandchild's life? A "parent" may be a neighbor. Somebody might have left a child outside. You know, I'm being honest. And that neighbor took their child because they didn't want that child in the welfare system. Their child now lives with the neighbor, you know. The District needed to recognize that reality. Again, why put up barriers?

I was also committed to keeping schools and teachers accountable. My thing is, how much are teachers involved? Cause, oh my God, we have children that are in kindergarten, first, second grade dropouts. They are. Cause they are doing nothing all day but roaming the halls and it's allowed. That is unacceptable for me. Yet, the adults in the schools allow it. When I say adults, I'm saying the parents and the teachers. And this was one of Dr. Ackerman's core beliefs. Children come first. Everything we do should be about the child. We had teachers who were supposed to be helping these children. There is too much foolishness going on in schools. I'm talking about adult foolishness. People come to work and are not working. And I'm not going to say this is every case, but it's in a lot of cases, especially in schools that are failing. Why do you think they are failing?

Something is going on in these schools, that they can't bring children up to yearly progress. There are some schools that are doing it right. Yes, it's the child. Yes, it is the child, but children are children. They don't even know what's going on. When I was a bus attendant, I saw this for myself. I was a one-on-one with this child as he went to his different classes. I went into this one teacher's class, they're sitting there doing their work. The whole class quiet, working. Then they go to the next teacher's class, with the same 30 students. Now, they're throwing papers. They're running around. They are cursing. That is not the children. That's the leader in that school and that classroom. That's classroom management, because if you got the same 30 children who are acting one way in this class and acting totally different in the next class, that ain't the children. Nobody's talking about that.

I'm just saying the teachers who are not doing their jobs, shouldn't have their jobs and get a check every two weeks. I mean, where can you go work, not do your job, and still get paid? It's foolishness. If a doctor keeps operating on people and every person he operates on dies, do you think that they going to let him keep his license? I don't think so. I think they will go, "Oh, we've got to call you in. You're doing something wrong, buddy." If a teacher continues to not educate children and is able to keep their job, I know they'll go, "Oh well it's not my fault. It's the children. They're five steps behind. They are not learning.

When we got them, they couldn't read and write." Okay, that's fine. But if you had the child in your school for six years and this child that started can't read and write, graduated at sixth grade, and still can't read and write, something needs to happen. Six years is a lot of time to be messing up somebody's life, a child's life. And to let it happen for twelve years? Come on. This is what we're doing in some neighborhood schools.

So I wanted real change. It's one thing to listen, then learn, then do. I had listened to parents. I had studied and learned. So I wanted to *do* big things for the children. Let's fucking put the brakes on this failing school district and shut it down. I said, "Let's just make all the schools *Promise Academies*[19]. Let's just take all the schools that are not serving children the way we wanted them to do. Let's make them all *Promise Academy* schools together." I thought that was a great idea. I did. I mean, if we're the School Reform Commission and Dr. Hite is the Superintendent, I don't understand why people worry about the Teachers' Union so much, who were against this move. Under the *Promise Academies*, people will still have their jobs. It's not like you're changing their jobs. I think that one of the problems is adults are afraid to make changes that might hurt other adults, even though it's beneficial to the children. I think this is why we have a lot of failing schools.

I remember when *Mastery Charter*[20] was trying to take over a District school. The parents came to me crying, saying their school is failing. They wanted something better. I listened to the families on both sides. And I put myself in their situation. I said, "Hmmm, I think *Mastery* will be a better option than what these children are getting now." So, I overrode Dr. Hite who wanted to turn the school around through the District. We chose a charter school instead. The families went into an uproar, but it was the unions that was causing it. It was the unions going up to the schools, telling the parents, "Keep your school a traditional public school." Then you had *Mastery Charter* up there saying "Change. Make a change. We want something new." It was the same thing with the *Steel Public School*. You had *Mastery* again going up there saying, "Oh we want to change *Steel*. "But then you had the parents saying, "We want to keep *Steel* a traditional public school." Unions are more concerned about teachers keeping their jobs than the children in the schools. And, today, it continues to fail even though they kept it a traditional public school.

To me, it's about, what are you doing for the children? I think that there's some people that are just for charter schools. That's all they want to do. They don't care if it's good or bad. That's what they are going to fight for. I think there are other people who are just for traditional public school. No matter how good or bad the public school is, this is what they are fighting for. To me, it doesn't matter whether it's a traditional public school or charter school. If you're not doing right, you've got to go. I'm unique in that I'll fight for any school that's doing good. But I'll rag on any school that's not performing. But again, when you get rid of a school, you take a whole lot into consideration. For me, it's like, where are those children going to go? My thing is I'd rather send my child to a failing school that is closer to me than to send my child to a failing school that is farther away. It's not like people are saying, "Oh, I'm going to close the school and I'm going to send you to this great school over here where you know your child would excel." No, you're sending my child to another failing school. That doesn't make sense to me. We need to focus less on moving children and more on fixing the schools. So, that's my spill on it.

I also think middle class parents can be part of the problem. I think what happens when you have a whole neighborhood of families that the system had failed there's a constant unspoken understanding: I went to this school. I wasn't educated. My mom went through the same schools and is on welfare. She wasn't educated. She don't know how to read and write. Now I'm sending my child to school. So as a mom, I wonder if my child is going to succeed. But I had to send my child to the neighborhood's failing school because I don't know how to navigate the system to get my child into a different school. Maybe if those parents start to organize, though, the school starts to improve. Then, when a school gets known as a great school that families in the neighborhood can get into, white people with a bit more money start moving into the neighborhood. So now, these original families can't get into school. And I said, "Why don't middle class families send y'all children to the failing neighborhood school, then that school will rise." There is no reason to move. It would be a win-win for everybody.

I think those middle-class white parents know how to navigate the system. They know that education is the key and want the best for their child. I'm not knocking it. I go to their meetings. I've talked to them. I always ask them "Why y'all coming into a Black neighborhood? How many Black people have you talked to?" None. It's always none. So you come into a neighborhood, pretty much taking over the elementary school. Some of them ain't even got no babies. But they know if they had a baby, they want their child to go to this school. So they start advocating for the school. They want to make sure the school is great for their child. Then they send the child there for pre-K so they can get in kindergarten, first, second. But as the grades get higher, they're taking their children out and putting them in better schools. I don't know where they send them. It's probably a charter school. It's probably a great charter school or great special admit school. Maybe the magnet schools. But what I notice in all situations is that my community doesn't have any resources by design. The more knowledge I get, the more I see things. The more it's like damn, stuff is geared for us to fail from the beginning, before we even get to the starting line. We are three steps behind, like our children. So it's like, who is looking out for us?

As a Commissioner, I didn't make it about a charter movement. I made it about the quality of the school your child is going to attend. And I think that may have been my downfall because, like I said, I don't like people to try to pit school against school. My thing is, if your school is doing a disservice to children, you don't need to be open. I don't care if it's a charter school or a traditional public school. If you're not doing what you're supposed to be doing as an educational entity, then bye. It doesn't matter. I don't care what type of school it is, just educate these babies. So for me, if you're failing, you got to go. I'm trying to give the parents more power in the schools, to make the schools more accountable.

This is why I wanted the School Advisory Councils to be able to fire their asses for not doing what they're supposed to be doing. It was a powerful tool. We just didn't use it. The School Advisory Council as an idea actually started, way back during Dr. Ackerman's time. It took like 12 years to make it a damn policy. We were working on it when Dr. Ackerman was here. It didn't get done until I was a commissioner on my way out. But at the end of the day, though, the decision was made to make it best for the principals, not the families, not the community, which was how it started out. We already know that principals have got the power, but everybody always wants to point fingers at parents and say, "You're not doing this. You ain't doing this for your child." To me, the School Advisory Councils were a way of giving parents more of a voice to be involved in their children's educa-tion. That could have been a way of holding parents accountable as well as making sure that their voices were at the table. With power comes responsibility.

To me, meaningful mutual engagement means having the respect to think that a parent voice is just as important as the leader's voice. You have to have that two way conversation and respect in order to make sure that things are going to go great. So for me, the two way meaningful conversation has respect for each other, even though you may disagree on things. That's why I thought engagement between the community and the school should happen through the School Advisory Council. It should be a true partnership, just everything should be about the child. If everybody is focusing on the child — the school, the parents and the families and the community — the child's going to be okay because everybody is making sure that their child is okay. That's partnership. A true partnership. Not just saying, "Oh, I have a partnership," but ignoring the fact that you really don't have a partnership.

We used to have a School Advisory Council at Ethel Allen School. That was where one of the first School Advisory Councils was created. It was really good when it was in effect, thanks to the great parents at that school. But what happened was when the parents got the power, they started looking down at other parents. I didn't like that cause it was like, we're the School Advisory Council. We are all the same. I think this looking down on people who are out of power happens because people don't want to share their power. They want to keep all the power for themselves. No matter if you're a parent, or an educator, or whoever. People want to keep their power. So, the parents on the Council start aligning themselves with the school administration and the School District. But I think if you're strong, you're not gonna let a principal intimidate you. Now you have to really be a strong parent to not be afraid of a principal or somebody in leadership because they'll try to intimidate you. They will try to use words that you don't understand. When I was appointed to the School Reform Commission, I didn't talk that talk, but I had to get to the point where I used to say in my head, "They dumb as shit." That way, I wouldn't fold. I wouldn't give in. I would go, "Motherfuckers don't do shit." My job is to speak for the poor parents, who they know nothing about.

I should also say that we don't have a School Advisory Council at my own school, which hurts my heart. I mean this was a policy we put into place while I was a commissioner. It's going to have one soon because when I left the School Reform Commission in June, I said that school is going to have a School Advisory Council. But why doesn't it have one? I'm not gonna say the principal doesn't want it. The principal wants it, but he wants to pick certain parents. He knows he doesn't want to lose control of his school. I love my principal and we have those crucial conversations. But I'm like "Principal, you've got to have parents on there who are not going to agree with you. You've got to have community partners on there that may not believe everything you say. Yes, we know you are the leader. Anything that happens is going to fall back to you. But if we are all working together, collectively, to make sure the school has everything it needs, we all have to be the leaders."

He's also in a very unique position. He has a former commissioner that is all up in his school. When I go in his school, he probably thinks, I'm going to be all up in his business. But I stay in my Family Engagement Center because I know when I walk the halls, people be like "ugh" thinking about themselves being watched, reported. But it ain't about them. What are we doing for these babies who live in my neighborhood? Cause like I said, they go to their little homes, they live in their own neighborhoods, but if these children don't get educated, these are going to be the same children who may be busting me upside my head. Going in my house and robbing me. I don't want to see that. I want to see these children become successful. Just because you live in a very impoverished neighborhood, doesn't mean you can't be successful. So I think when people see me in the school, they go, "Damn, we're fucking up." I think that's why people don't want me around because I'm going to remind you. "Yes, you're still fucking up. You know, we got to do better. We've got to do better."

Whatever decision I have made, though, whatever I do, I can always look at myself in the mirror and be happy. Even at my lowest of lows. 'Cause to be honest, right now, this is my lowest of lows. I really haven't been doing my organizing because I need a job right now. So if you're fighting, if you see things that your families need, and you can't help, it hurts. I still talk to them. I still talk to my parent leaders all the time. A lot of times we just be like, "Damn, we fucked up. We've got to do the work." You know, and I'm sitting up here going, "Shit I haven't paid my damn electric bill." And they are going, "We know Syl. We also struggling." So one of them went back on social security, the other one has a husband that, before I gave her the job, the husband was taking care of the home. The other one had their own business. And while me and my parents are having to find ways to pay bills instead of organizing, the non-profits that *work* for the community, they're doing fine. They're getting paid. It's me that's still poor. It's my neighbors who are still poor.

In my heart of hearts, I know I am doing the right thing by staying committed. I know the Creator will make sure that I'm okay. I know this is a test. I'm going through this test. I believe in my heart that I'm going to pass. I do. But I don't know why. I ask myself, 'cause I've been going through some stuff. I ask myself, "Why is this happening to me? Why is this happening to my parents?" I don't know. You know, even though I say I got the power, there's a higher being than me. Whatever is meant for me is going to be for me. People cannot stop that. I do know that no matter what, people can try to blackball you, they can try to put barriers in front of you, but at the end of the day, I believe that what is meant for you, will be for you.

So I'm coming back, y'all. I'm coming back. Because like I said, I am the families that I serve. And it's hard for me to be getting back and forth down to the District sometimes. Cause I ain't got cab fare. And sometimes I feel as though I'm blackballed since leaving the School Reform Commission because I know too much. I know a lot. I know that the district is doing a disservice to a lot of families. We are losing too many children. And the children that we are losing are the poor children. Poor. It's not a Black or white thing. Poor. It's class. We are losing children because families don't know how to navigate the system. The families don't know what they don't know, whether they are poor white families, poor Asian families, poor Latino families, poor Black families … poor. So I always go back and help people. I'm always looking out for others instead of looking out for Sylvia. I don't know if there's something that I have to learn or should I even continue to fight. I mean, do I still want to help people? Yes. I want to always help them because they need help.

I'm just saying I'm not going anywhere. Until y'all fix my schools in my community, I'm not going anywhere. I'm not.

Chapter 6
"If you're not listening to everybody . . . you're doing yourself a disservice to the cause."

As a parent advocate, you're watching every second. Now, you might not see everything, but you will see a lot. That's why systems are so afraid of parents being involved because we'll see what's going on. It's just like being a parent who is concerned about their child. If I have a child that's struggling, I'm at the school every day. I can see what really goes on. I see children walking in our halls all day. I see teachers lollygagging, not teaching. Parents coming up there acting crazy. So when you are in the school all day, every day, you see what's going on. Then you can go, "Wow, this is a mess."

But just because you can see it and report it, doesn't mean the school will listen to you. This is the important difference with *PARENT POWER*. We serve all families, but we really try to target those families who people don't even talk to. We try to help them, teach them what they don't know, wake them up to their power. And when all these parents wake up, do you think things are going to be the same? No. You're going to see a change. You're going to see massive change. The parents are going to say, "No more. Not on my watch."

That's what *Title 1* was meant to be about — eliminating barriers, changing how things are. Schools get all of this money from the federal government to eliminate barriers, but you know what schools do instead? They make the barriers higher. They make them higher and nobody talks about the barriers. And when you talk about them, you get ignored. Federal law, state law, both say every school district has to put together a family and community engagement policy. But that could be dangerous to the status quo. The District is so weak on engagement because the State lets it be weak on family engagement. The State just gives schools a template and says, "Fill in the blanks."

So I said, let's put together a real policy. Let's use the District's *Title One Parent Advisory Council*, which was made up of *PARENT POWER* members, to make a real policy. See, we had been coming to the *Title 1* meetings regularly. We dug deep within the District and outside of the District because we didn't believe everything the District was saying. We noticed in the law, and we noticed it in a lot of laws, lawmakers always give leeway. For instance, where it might need to be "have to," the lawmaker will write the law to say "shall." "The district shall do." Then the District interprets that as meaning, "Oh, the district may do this, the district can do this." So every requirement becomes a "shall" instead of a "have to."

PARENT POWER was trying to make it so there wasn't any choice. We want the district to do everything that they were supposed to be doing. They fought us on that. Even when I was a Commissioner, they fought me on it. And even today, the district does not have a *Title One Parent Advisory Council*. The law said the district "may" have a *Title One Parent School Advisory Council*. That's a may. So, in fact, it's a "may not." And I know when bullshit is bullshit. So I'm going, "Here they go again." They didn't want parents to know how to navigate the system, to know how to go against the system, to know how to help their children. Even though they said they wanted parents to know. They're bullshitting.

That's why, to me, it's always interesting that people in power always say they want to end poverty. People always say they want to create better schools. People always say they want to build better cities. They want to make a better United States. But people don't fund or help low income families. They don't fund parent organizing. I think they realize, "Wow, If we fund these parents, then they're going to have the power, and we won't have the power to control them." I mean, the majority of the people are getting screwed over. I sit at a lot of tables with non-profit leaders. Do people really have the crucial conversations about what we are doing here? Who are we here to serve? What is our mission? What is our vision? What do we really want to do? Nope. Because they don't want to hear it. They really don't.

68

Everywhere I go, I have conversations, but I'm the minority. So is anyone listening to Sylvia or the needs of her community? No. I mean that honestly. I feel that way. Maybe, they *listened* to me, but they didn't *act*.

I don't see large non-profits actually helping much. To me, they are getting paid so they can continue living their good lives. I had a conversation with a woman at a non-profit the other day. I was telling her that everybody wants to ask me how I engage families because, they say, "I'm doing it right," even though I have few resources. There are people who are getting millions and hundreds of thousands of dollars and are not doing it the way we're doing it. They talk their shit. They know buzz words. They know what to say. They're connected to somebody else. They want change but they don't want to pay poor people, like my *PARENT POWER* parents, who know how to create *real* change. This is the treatment I and my parents receive from the white progressives. They treat me like . . . Well, I won't use the word, but you know what I mean.

The sad thing, and I'm gonna say it, is a lot of disrespect also came from Black female principals. It really did. And it is going on to this day. I don't know if they feel as though they have "made it" and look down on Black female parents. Maybe they just don't value us, which is sad. This is not only from my experience. I hear this from my parents' experiences too. A lot of my parents who are in the struggle, a lot of them have the most problems with Black female principals. I think these principals believe parents are ignorant and don't have any values. Some of them actually know what our parents are going through be-cause some of them were us. You have people who used to live in poverty, were on welfare, got their college degrees, and became successful. They don't want to remember where they came from. What is it with our Black female principals that they don't value Black parents?

That hurts me, too. I've been hurt a lot. People have done me dirty. I think non-profits want me on their panels and com-mittees because number one, I'm Black. Two, I'm low income. But when I get there and the same folks go, "Oh, snap. This girl may be Black and without a college degree, but she knows her stuff." My education is from the school of hard knocks. That doesn't get them to listen to me though. Any position that I had, I never felt respected. And that's their loss. It's their loss because, look, I'm Sylvia P. Simms; I can't fix the world, but I do have something to add on to the world. My parents also have something to add to the world. I think a lot of times folks on these commissions only know what they know, but they don't listen to new information, new ideas. Everyone who sits there has something unique to bring to the table. I know the families that we're supposed to be serving. I know the children. But if you're not listening to everyone who's at the table, whether you agree or disagree with them, then you're doing yourself a disservice to the cause.

To me, this is like me renovating a house. Now I didn't build my house. I just bought new windows. And you come in and say, "Oh Sylvia, I love what you're doing here. I'm going to buy you some windows." And I go, "I don't need windows. Can you buy me some new floors?" And you go, "Nope, I'm going buy you windows." And I go, "I don't need windows, I need floors. Can you give me some floors?" And you go, "No, I'm buying you windows." So either I'll get better windows for myself, or I'll say, "No, I don't want your windows." So maybe I take the windows. Then they go, "We gave her windows. Now she better do whatever we tell her to do." That's what goes on.

I'm not saying boo to people who have degrees. I say right on, you're good. But what I think is that for every person who has a degree, your best friend should be somebody who doesn't. That way you could do the check and balance. Because you don't know everything. They don't know everything. Somewhere you can meet in the middle. People get in these positions and they get these titles, then they forget why they're supposed to be there. And I think this is why Philadelphia, Pennsylvania, and the United States, are where we are. For me, with funders and non-profits, it's like, "You don't know everything, either." We need the people who *think they know everything* to start talking to the people who they think *don't know anything*. That's the crucial conversations that a lot of folks don't want to have. And when two people start sitting at a table and listening, it becomes a moment when, "Let us say what we have to say, you all say what you all to say, and hopefully some way we can meet in the middle to make this work."

Low-income people are not ignorant. We're not dumb. Just because we may live in poverty, it doesn't mean that's where we want to be. I think a lot of times, these organizations that get lots of funding miss that point. The worst thing that they can do is to not have people working for them who know the community being served. I think that's the worst thing big organizations do. They never want to pay that Black person, that parent, who's in that community. They don't want to pay that community organizer their actual worth like they would pay somebody who has a college degree. I think at one time people saw each other's worth. But I think the system has made it where if you don't have a college degree, then you don't have any worth. I really think that system is the one that is keeping people in poverty, keeping folks where they want them to be so they can be successful.

I guess I don't see why this happens. Because, as I see it, what have the non-profits done? What has the district done? What have we done? Children still can't read and write. Our communities are still messed up. So really, what have we done? You know, we sit on these boards, we sit on these committees, we sit on these things and when you look, you see, "Children can't read!" I'm not pointing a finger at any one particular person. It's a society thing. Until we are all willing to change – and I'm talking about massive change, I'm not talking about little, teeny change here and there, it will always be that way — our children are not being educated. But I believe, I really believe, that change can happen. I think anything can be undone that was done if people have the balls to do it. Will it take a lot of time? Yes, but it took a lot of time for it to get to be a mess. But why not try to begin to fix it now and make it better?

Again, I think there's a lot of people who don't want it done, because if it's done, a lot of people aren't going to have jobs. They want to keep their jobs. I think a lot of stuff is tied to other folks' positions and other folks' jobs. And I'm going tell you what else they do that we, as the parents, allow. Every time the district assigns a new Parent Administrator, they want to bring in their own parents. So it's like you the parents who have been around, who know how to navigate the system, are out. "We don't want you, get out." And they put up things to make you leave. Like not letting you know when meetings are, not telling you different things, not letting you go on trips cause you're not "their" parent. It becomes about how to keep power, not change how power works.

It goes back to the haves and the have nots. If you have everything and I don't have anything, then if you help me, then your mindset goes, "Dang, if I help Sylvia, then she might be where I'm at or may pass me." I think that's what a lot of people fear. But I always tell people, "What's meant for Sylvia is for Sylvia. I'm not taking nothing away from you. I'd probably help us both to be successful, because if you know what you know and I know what I know, and we communicate with each other, that's going to lift everybody up." I really think that we have so much work to do. And until the people who have got power and wealth start sharing it with the folks who do not have it, poverty is going to continue. We need to come to where we can meet in the middle.

What I see in Philadelphia, though I know it is broader than Philadelphia, is that society is about the haves and the have-nots. If I don't have, I'm going to continue to struggle. Even if I get out a little bit, I'm still struggling. The people over here, the haves, they know how to navigate the system. They know how to talk their talk. They know how to walk their walk. They know how to be connected. They know what circles people are in. If you know how to navigate the system and you're able to get out, you'll go. If I became rich, would I get up and leave my community? No. I'm not *The Jeffersons*. What I would do is build my community. The first thing I would do is put in a *Family Engagement Center* somewhere. I would buy a house and put in a *Family Engagement Center*. That's what I would do.

What makes me upset is how there are folks out here who are getting money for nothing. There are great people doing great work. Then there are some people who are doing nothing. And we know who those people are, but they continue to get funded because they have the hook up. The hook up is you're the executive director or the board chair of an organization that's giving out money to people. Say, I have a non-profit or for-profit, and you're my girlfriend. So you'll go, "Hey, I'm going to give Sylvia some money" even knowing Sylvia isn't doing anything. Knowing Sylvia isn't really helping these people, hasn't seen a parent in years. But I'm going to give her money, because that's giving my friend a job.

People see the work I'm doing. They see it, and they know it, because people know me. People know my work. They see the parents. It's on social media when we get together, what we're doing. That's why a lot of times I don't even post anything anymore because, "Screw you. You aren't giving us anything anyway. If you're giving us anything, you're giving us crumbs because you don't want us to be successful." And I'm really starting to believe people are not helping me, not helping organizations like PARENT POWER, because if they help me, then they know I'm going to help and work for others. And I don't think anyone wants the change that might follow from that.

Chapter 7
"That's Our Families Being Killed in the Neighborhoods."

I've seen a lot of deaths. A lot of friends, friends of my girlfriends and people who I worked with have died. On August 1, 2005, my mom passed away. We had already planned a trip to go to New Orleans. We were going the end of August. When my mom passed away, we were like, "Oh shit. Should we go? Should we stay?" Finally we decided to go. It was me, my three sisters, my two daughters, and one of my sister's girlfriends who went.

Now, remember there was no hurricane when we got there, New Orleans was beautiful. Everything was beautiful. I think we were there for three days and then we heard that the hurricane was coming. We were tourists and were doing things, you know, having fun. We go into this program where they were teaching us how to cook New Orleans food. It lasted maybe two hours. When we came out from the class, we saw that people had boarded up their stores and everything. We figured, well what? We asked the people, "Has a hurricane hit before? What happens?" They were like, "Oh nothing." So we just kept on doing our thing... We were totally surprised to see everything boarded up because those we had spoken to were so nonchalant.

We also see some brothers. We were like, "Well it's a hurricane coming. What y'all gonna do?" We were talking to them. And they were like, "Well, they send everybody down to the Super Dome. So, that's where everybody's going. So we want to go down there. We're gonna steal. We're gonna take their stuff. We're gonna take their luggage. We're gonna do that." The brother was like, "If I was y'all, I wouldn't go down to the Super Dome." So that's why we walked back and went to the hotel. We were gonna ride it out in the hotel.

When we got back to the hotel, that's when people started calling us. They're seeing all this stuff on TV. We ain't see nothing. We don't know nothing because the electricity went out once the hurricane hit. Before we left, the weather said there was going to be a hurricane in Florida, but they didn't say nothing about New Orleans. So that's why we went. Ain't no hurricane coming to New Orleans, so, you know, we go. But now we getting all these phone calls. Everybody was worried about us. We started to think maybe we should prepare ourselves.

We all got together and were like, "Okay. We are going to put our beds against the window. We are going to fill the tub up with water." We were in survival mode. Our vibe was: we're not dying. Then, the hurricane came, and we survived it. But what happened was that the levees broke. I looked out of my room window and I saw this big, big, big, black mushroom cloud. So, to me, it was like something was blown up or on fire. That's when people started getting really panicked. We had a meeting at the hotel with management and guests. The hotel management was like, "We gonna get y'all out safely," talking all this stuff.

Several days passed. We were getting low on food. The hotel was still trying to feed us. We had our own water. We had our own non-perishable food. And being me, I was running places and snatching cereal, and other food. I was in survival mode for me and my family. So, then, management got us all together again. They were saying that we had to evacuate the hotel. That everybody had to leave. But of course, we didn't have anywhere to go. All the train stations were closed. All the airports were closed. Everything was closed. Remember, we didn't have any working phones because the electricity was gone.

After the meeting, they were still feeding us until we left. They gave us these eggs. And I tell you, I was like, I'm not dying like this. I'm not. Because the eggs was supposed to be boiled eggs. But when you cracked them, they were nasty. I'm not eating this stuff! So I got upset and started to cry. I'm like "No! I'm not eating this stuff. I'm not dying like that." So, I left my family and I went out and roamed the hotel for food. I found out the hotel was having a private meeting with all the hotel workers. The food and beverage man was saying "Oh, we gotta get out. We gonna do what we gonna do." They were leaving us to fend for ourselves. So, there were two meetings: the meeting that they had with the hotel guests, and the meeting that they had with the hotel staff. I happened to go into the room with the hotel staff. And they were just telling them, "Y'all better go. Y'all better get out of here."

Now, remember, I'm not in the room because I'm separated from my family. So, I'm like, "Oh my God. Man, I gotta find my family." So I was running up and down the steps, trying to find my family. Once I found my family and we were all back together, we go outside. This is where money comes in. People with big vans were coming in to take people out. Drivers were taking money from people. They told us they wanted $100 a head. There were seven of us. But, because I have sisters and they're big-boned women, he was like, "I can't take all y'all, because my shocks are not gonna support everybody." So we had to separate. My daughter, Skeetia, was already in the van. So, I'm like, listen, put Allegra, my other daughter, in the van with y'all, and I'll stay back. So we sitting there going, okay, who else is going in the van? And I said to my oldest sister, "Deb, you gotta go in the van." My sister had cancer and she was medically fragile. Now there are three in the van. So we still looking, cause I'm like, I know I'm staying back — save my two children first. I was looking around, and saying, "Okay, who's next? Who else is gonna go in the van?" So Donna, my youngest sister said, "Well, I'll stay back." And since she stayed back, her girlfriend said, "Imma stay back, with Donna."

So, I told Quibila, "You've got to go, you've got to take care of my kids just in case I don't make it." So we did a whole little, "You and I will never part." They had video cameras so we're on videotape crying. "I love y'all, we love..." You know, cause we didn't know what was gonna happen. Then they drove off. Me and my sister and her girlfriend just stayed behind. I said to my sister, "You're gonna hear some things that you never heard your sister say, out of her mouth. But trust me, we're gonna get outta here." Cause, I ain't letting my baby sister die, she's getting out of there. That's my baby sister, you know what I'm saying?

So, we were outside the hotel, trying to get a ride. When people drove past, we were waving down cars. It got crazy. I tell you people were riding past people, honestly. They had dogs and cats in their cars and were leaving the humans behind. I was like, you got to be kidding me. Ain't nobody stopping. Everybody's going. Then I see the hotel food and beverage man in his truck. Baby, I stopped that van. I put my body in front of that truck. I said, "I was in that room where you said that everybody in this hotel was gonna get out safely. We ain't out. You ain't going nowhere." He was like, "Ma'am, just get in. Just get in." He had one of those pick-up trucks with only three seats. So, my sister and her girlfriend got inside of the van. I got in back of the pick-up. He's driving. We don't know where we're going. I don't know where my sister and daughters are in the other van, because we didn't have service on our phones. They were dead because we didn't have electricity. Like I said, everybody's phone was dead.

I found out we were heading past the Convention Center. When we first got to New Orleans and saw the Convention Center, it was so nice and beautiful. When we saw it after the hurricane, it was covered by water and I couldn't fathom it. My body shut down. Because I didn't know what else was ahead. My body shut down. I saw the devastation and my body went, "I'm out." When I woke up, the first thing I did was look, to make sure my sister and her friend were still in the van. Then, we kept driving toward the Baton Rouge Airport. We were still riding when I looked up... what do I see? My children. They were saying, "MOM! MOM!" That was the best thing, cause a lot of people couldn't find their families. They didn't know what happened to their families. You understand? After we were together and we rented two vans to Houston, Texas, from there, we caught a plane to Philadelphia. It was great to get back home.

Looking back, I'm not sure how it impacted me. To be honest, being poor and living in the hood, I had already seen things. You know, I had seen people get their head blown off when I was a little child. At 18 years old, I noticed the difference between the number of people who die in other people's friend circles compared to my circle of friends. Right? Like, there's just, more. When my daughter was younger, she had a lot of friends who were murdered. And I'm quite sure that that had an impact on her. I don't know if it still does, it may still. You don't know what people have buried. That's our blood being spilled in the neighborhoods. I think this is what is happening to our children now. They see things, they keep it moving. I wonder if it affects them, how it affected me.

After Hurricane Katrina, we saw that the people of New Orleans knew how to survive. When I was there, I saw the people of the city fight to survive. And I realized again that my community knows how to survive too. I gain strength from being around them. Even though they're living in poverty, living through violence, they're the happiest people. Honestly. When I look at the people on my block—and I'm going to just use the people on my block and my community, because that is where I live and that's who I know for the most part—a lot of them, they don't have a care in the world. Honestly. They're just doing them. They're doing the best that they can do with what they have. You never see them walking around going, "Woe is me." You never hear them jumping out of a window committing suicide, even though they have a bad hand. A lot of them are on welfare, living in Section 8 housing, or barely paying their rent. A lot of them are really, really struggling. They are the strongest people I know. And I admire them all.

As a community, they know everybody here is going to protect them. Nobody's going to hurt them. So that's where their freedom comes from. Even though a lot of them don't work, a lot of them are on welfare, they're happy, because they don't picture or imagine themselves somewhere else. And I used to be them. I was on welfare, I used to live in my own little zone, in my little bubble. I've done a lot since then, but I didn't leave my community because when you know your people in your community, you know they're going to protect you by any means necessary. They're going to have your back. They're going to ride with you. I've been here all my life. Moved and came back. I love them all. And they've been my fight. My cause. We survive.

Chapter 8
"If You're Not at the Table, You're on the Menu."

I didn't know much about politics. When I started *PARENT POWER*, I knew that there would be politics involved. As I said earlier, what really blew up *PARENT POWER* was when I started taking pictures with different politicians and people in leadership. People were like, "Oh, she's with different city council people." Then, when I was first on the School Reform Commission, I was just so impressed, like "Wow. I'm sitting next to these big people!" But as you get embedded in this work, you see they're nothing but people. They're people just like you and I, but they're people with power. They can make decisions. They can make political change if they choose. I think that's the root of my frustration.

I wasn't even going to take the School Reform Commission position because I would have to give up my position as a committee person in the city's Democratic Party. For whatever reason, a lot of people think that the committee person seat is so powerful because the committee people vote for the ward leader. And then the ward leader picks who they want to support for city council or state representative or state senator. That's where the real power comes. What I learned was that at every moment, the real battle is people are jockeying for power, not for the people. I learned what happens is that people get in powerful positions, and they forget about the people they're serving. Maybe at first their main focus was the people, but when they get to where they are going, that vanishes. There are so many other opportunities that they're not really connected to the people anymore. Now, they're just connected with people who think like them. And I really think that's what happens a lot. Not with everyone, but with a lot of people in power.

When I became a commissioner, even though I was with powerful people, I still tried to be with my community. Even today, after being on the School Reform Commission, I have a little summer camp for the children on my street through the Play Street program, that is a program where you close off your street from 10:00 a.m. to 4:00 p.m. Nobody can drive up the street unless they live there or are making deliveries. I did that because I have a really small street and people drive it like it's a highway. And when I used to live at my old house, one of my neighbor's children got killed by a car zooming down the street. I didn't want a repeat of that on my street.

I also added a lunch program. One thing I realized when I was a commissioner was that many children do not eat during the summer. So in my last year as commissioner, I added a lunch and snack program. On a good day, we hand out 30 lunches. In fact, when I went on vacation, my nephew and some of his friends covered the summer lunch program. I was like, this is what you got to do. Every time you give a child a lunch, you got to number it. So now, they know what to do and how to do it. These are what some people may consider the "bad boys." They ain't bad to me, though. These are my neighbors. These are my guys. Yesterday, was very, very hot. I was having hot flashes and my body was just overheating. I didn't want to be outside, so I asked one of the guys, "Could you do the lunch for me?" And he was like, "Yeah." He didn't really know what to do, so I told him. After that he was like, "All right." It made him feel good because he knows he was out there helping children that day. We also get the guys to play volleyball or tag with the children. I'm talking about the men and the young brothers on our block. It's everybody coming together.

We give out books to the children from the Read by 4th program[21]. We do literacy workshops with the parents and their children. We actually engage the families. The good thing is, the more workshops we do, the more parents join in our activities. That's the beauty of doing what I do. When I grab a parent and say, "I'm Sylvia, I want to help," I'm helping parents to help themselves, so they can help improve their children's lives. Because honestly, that's what it's about. We don't want to have a continuance of families in poverty. And I do know now that education is the key out of poverty.

We also provide trips. We've been to the *Philadelphia Zoo, The Academy of Natural Science, The Franklin Institute,* and *Please Touch Museum.* We took children to the Camden Aquarium. They love that because they actually go on a ferry to get to the aquarium. We take them to the park. We visited the *Wawa Festival.* The trips allow them to see a different side of life. Sometimes we just stay on the block and play games. And it's so good because the neighbors come out to help and support us. We get some grants. Senator Street gave us money to pay for trips, materials, and books. But really, I'm just paying for all this out of my own pocket and my house is open to everyone. Folks just come in and take stuff from the refrigerator. So really, it's me.

This is what I mean about politicians leaving their community or just acting like they support the community when it's really about themselves. Like, it used to be that the community gave out book bags, bikes, coats. Now the council people and state reps are giving these out instead. Now they can say, "Look, I gave you a coat. I gave you poor people a book bag. I'm looking out for you." But they haven't challenged the power that hurts the neighborhood. They haven't supported the programs and people who are making a change in the neighborhood. They don't want the community saying "Thank you Syl. Wow. *PARENT POWER* gave me a coat when my children ain't have no coats." That would give the community a sense of their own power to take care of themselves. That might mean they have the power to challenge the politicians.

Since the community doesn't know it has power, politicians are able to be loyal to those who give them money, like the unions. For a long time, I didn't know how detrimental unions were in the politics. When I saw it, I mean when I actually got up and saw it, I was like "Oh Lord," they ain't doin' shit." I'm serious. Sad to say, but my thing is, if I give you thousands and thousands of dollars to win, you have to be loyal to me. The teachers' union usually votes for Democrats, so the Democratic Party is never critical of the District or the teachers' union. So, everything the District does is supported by the unions. You can't do nothing in damn schools unless you get the union's approval. If I wanted to go in my child's classroom and paint, we'd have to go through a whole damn thing just to paint the doors of every classroom. In fact, we can only do it on Martin Luther King Day 'cause unions got painters and nobody can paint the school but them. So, they would rather see the school not painted than to be painted by somebody in the community. Again, adult foolishness.

I have had several meetings with the President of the teachers' union. I remember he said to me, "I don't pick the teachers, the district does. It's my job to protect them." And I said, "Wow, do you protect bad people who are not doing their jobs?" I think that's what I want to know: Are you protecting bad behavior? If you know people are not doing what they're supposed to do in a classroom, as a human being, as an advocate for children, you need to say, "You are a very nice person, but this job is not for you." Even our Superintendent has said to me on several occasions, "We got a lot of bad principals. These principals are horrible." He has said that to me on several occasions. Well, why are they still there? If you know you have horrible people and you're not doing anything to make them better, maybe you need to tell them, "This job is not for you." That's a leader. And I don't see a lot of people leading. If folks are not doing their job and people know they are not doing their job, I would rather they have nobody in that position. The money we are paying that person could be used for another resource.

I'm disappointed with Democrats because they don't fight. They go in with the "all get along" idea. I don't think they want change. I think they want to keep it status quo and keep their jobs 'cause it's about their power. Same with the Republicans. Both sides are just people and people want to control their future, so they are just doing things that are gonna benefit them. We know that there are people out here that're doing a disservice to poor people and they don't need to be in that job, that office. And when I look at it as a whole, I look at the Democratic Party, I look at the Republican Party, and I don't see them want to make real change.

I've thought about running for City Council or State Representative, but you have to have money and I don't have the money needed. In fact, almost no poor person could afford to run for office. This shows that the city, as a government, needs to start focusing more of its time on the poor communities and less on supporting those who already have money or power. And it needs to recognize that we have different levels of poor people. I'm poor, but I'm not on welfare poor, okay? So, a person that's on welfare, may go, "Sylvia, you're not poor, because you look good, you come out here, you know…" So, people don't look at me as if I'm poor, but I'm poor. So, the people that's next to me, that's working making money, they're poor, too. You also have working class poor. There are different levels of poor people. It all depends on how you see yourself. But the city isn't addressing the many types of poverty.

So, if I was a politician, first and foremost, I would feel the need to address poverty. I think that there's a lot of poverty in Philadelphia. First, you have to listen to the people who are living in poverty and once you listen to them, you have to address their concerns, because addressing their concerns is going to change poverty. If people tell me, "Sylvia, yes, I get food stamps, but I have to pay my rent. So, I have to sell my food stamps to live in a house." Okay, as a political leader, I would make sure I have a food shelter in my community. If people are saying, "I don't have any money to buy Pampers or formula," or whatever, I would have a community center in my neighborhood. Like I said, even though you might not change things at once, you can help people with their needs and I think this is what people are not doing. And it's not only elected officials. I think people that are in power are not really listening to the needs and concerns of poor people.

I would have monthly community meetings with my people so I could understand their lives. I think, a lot of times, people don't feel heard. I would show respect by listening to them. Even if you cannot help people, if you just listen to them, listening goes a long way. I would also hold monthly meetings with the block captains of the neighborhood. I would want to meet with the committee people of the neighborhood. I would try to have a good relationship with the ward leader. I would meet with them about their concerns. I think what happens is, people who are in positions to make change are afraid to make change, because of the politics of everything. So, in talking to the people that I serve, I would meet with them, have critical conversations, build strong alliances, so we can address the community's concerns.

If I were to start a non-profit to support communities, I would make sure that the Executive Director had to have a Community Advisor who was poor, living in poverty. In terms of school, these might be seen as uneducated people but they are really the smartest people in the world. They'll teach you things that you didn't even think about. And when I say hire someone from a poor community, I'm not talking about folks from the Neighborhood Action Councils[22], you know those little pocket of people who have learned how to navigate the system. I'm not talking about them. They speak for the people, but they have learned how to navigate the system. Non-profits need someone who can skip past that and go straight to the people who are truly alienated.

There would be two immediate benefits for addressing poverty if non-profits were to hire this type of community member. Number one, they're going to help that person get out of poverty, because they're going to give them a job. That would bring hope because impoverished people want better. Listen, a crack head doesn't wake up saying, "I want to be a crack head." Something happened to make them become a crack head, or on opioids, or any drug of choice. People want better for themselves, even when sometimes, they don't know how to go about getting better. Shit, even drug dealers, they're businessmen. They're not dumb. They just happen to be on the corner selling drugs, because they can't find a job, because they may have a criminal record. But, they're businessmen. They're not going to go work for $8.00 an hour when they are out here hustling all day. So, low-income people have knowledge they can bring to an organization that a lot of people who are far removed from them don't know. If non-profits want to support a community, they can do so by actually hiring the people in that community.

I mean hire real people who have to stay involved and continue to live in the community. Just like politicians, there is a danger that when you hire somebody, as they continue to elevate, they forget why they got into their position in the first place. They get puffed up with pride. They start getting removed or getting into a different clique of elitist people. As a member of the community, I wouldn't let them forget where they came from, so that way they would continue fighting and uplifting more people. If they started to abandon their community, I would have in depth conversations. I'm not going to let people forget because we ain't never going to leave the community. So, we're not going to become successful and then move into Center City or on City Line Avenue or in King of Prussia. We're going to become successful and we're going to stay in the neighborhood. We could start buying up the homes, building wealth in the community that we serve. You know what I'm saying?

The second benefit from hiring local people is that the Community Advisor would bring knowledge of that community. They might know some stuff about the community already, but they would also go ask the people in the neighborhood what is needed. Now, a community is not going to tell a stranger everything they need because they're going to be embarrassed. That's why I do the food lunches and stuff. They're not telling me, but I already know they need it. So, there's going to be some things that they're not going to tell a stranger, but, in building relationships with folks, that's what makes people comfortable to talk and tell you what they need. They will trust community members more than outside experts from unknown non-profits. One of the things community advisors can do is to give you a peek into the community that non-profit leaders can't usually access, access to the families that they are supposed to be serving.

See, I think non-profits should build their programs by talking to the community. Ask them. I think the community knows what they need, but because the system had just negated them for so many years, it's like, they believe nobody will listen. People want help building safe space in their neighborhoods because a lot of people, like my neighborhood, don't have anywhere for the children to play. Now, we have a recreation center across the street from us, but that's not *our* recreation center. I live on the border line between Councilman Darrell Clarke and Councilwomen Cindy Bass' districts. And as a Cindy Bass constituent, I don't feel comfortable crossing the street and going into a Darrell Clarke center. It's a whole different turf and neighborhood. Not to say that children don't go there, because we do go over there, but it's Darrell Clarke's recreation center. So, where I live at, the closest recreation center to me is blocks away. And when I say blocks, I'm saying major streets. Maybe five. So, where I live in my community, in my neighborhood, we have nothing. We have no libraries. We have no recreation centers. We have no resource center, except the one that we built inside the school. So when I tell you in my community that we have nothing, we have nothing. I think every community should have a library, a rec center, and a resource center. There should be equality across all neighborhoods.

Now, I know a community may get more because they have a big voting bloc. And in my community, people don't come out and vote, so that's why we don't get anything. After years of folks not voting, the community is going to get fewer resources. I think that if you have a city council seat, your goal should be to not worry about who votes; you should be worried about going to the poor communities to build libraries, recreation centers, resource centers. That's not happening now. I mean, poor people don't vote because nobody's going to care about poor people whoever wins, anyway. So, why should I take my time, get out and go vote, when no matter who I vote for, they're not going to care? It's like, damned if you do, damned if you don't. Politicians need to show they care about everyone before they can expect everyone to vote. That's their job.

My non-profit would also teach about systems, teach people how to navigate systems to create change, get benefits. I don't think poor people have been taught how bureaucratic systems work. And I didn't either, until I got caught up in it. I knew the District, I knew they were full of it, but it wasn't until I got into it that I knew how systems really work. And even though I was in it for four years, I still don't understand why it takes so long to do things. I always just say, "Listen, if I'm a Commissioner... Do it!" But change takes balls. And I think people in power often don't have balls because they're worrying about other stuff. They're afraid of change, so they won't make change. I would want to teach people in my community how systems work and how to help themselves in life. Because systems have to be changed.

This is where I think the education of poor people comes into play. If people knew better, they could do better. You know, Harriet Tubman said she, "could have freed more slaves if they knew they were slaves." We need to see how the school system is damaging our children. To do that, we need to have information, to know the system. But the district doesn't share information, so people in poor communities don't know how the system works. So they're ignored by the district since they don't know how to make the district listen to them. When I started *PARENT POWER*, we got so organized, that we knew how systems work, we knew what the fight was, we knew what the issues were. But because we were poor and Black, nobody listened to us. But they knew, we were talking truth. But if politicians and non-profit leaders made sure people had a living wage, and safety nets, you couldn't do that to them. By hiring people from the community in non-profits, supporting their needs, non-profits could give communities the stability that will let poor people really organize to change systems.

But that's why most organizations don't want to help poor people. They know that if they share information with poor communities or if they fund organizations that are really going to help the poor people organize, these folks will not be afraid to change a system that doesn't benefit them. Trust and believe, I think that when you have people funding "parent work," that if you start doing too much of what the people in power don't want, they're going to come and say, "Hey, don't do that." Or, "If you do that again, you ain't going to get no money." So, maybe I say, "I don't care, I don't want your money. I'm going to do this for the people." But then, next year my organization is gone, because I went against the people who were funding. Folks need jobs. As a result, I have seen a lot of my parents getting picked off working for the district with job offers. Once you work for the district, you become part of the system, so now you can't advocate the way you could when you were outside, because you need your paycheck. But you are one voice among 200,000. If *PARENT POWER* could pay the parents, they'd probably stay outside the system. That's why I would have my non-profit hire the alienated folks, who are not benefitting from the system. They are the ones that will change it.

Right now, I'm helping to teach a college course at Temple University for future teachers, future principals. When I was asked to come teach, I was like, "I just don't really feel like it, I just don't." But then I said, "Well, half of these people may not know what poverty is or what being poor is." So, they get to see it first-hand. I get to share my story with them and hope that if they see somebody that's less fortunate than them, then maybe they will not look down on them. Maybe they will learn to talk to the parents who understand the community, their children — how these parents understand the needs in the way that an outsider never could. Hopefully, these future teachers and principals will make better decisions. I mean, poor communities have seen people come and go, come and go, come and go. We're still here. So why not listen to us? I'm just saying, why not? I mean, no one of us is as smart as all of us!

Maybe they will learn to stand up for the children, not the adults. For example, there's a lot of good teachers and good principals, but then there's a lot of ones who go with the status quo. But if you are a teacher, if you're walking through the hallway, and you see one of your colleagues hollering at a child, don't just turn your head. After the situation is over, go and say something to that teacher, because nobody would want an adult talking to their child like that. You wouldn't want anybody screaming at your child in a classroom, so why would you do that to somebody else's child? Maybe they can see that if, as a parent, you see teachers running out the door when the bell rings, they might wonder why teachers can't stay a little longer. Or ask what's wrong with going outside and helping the noontime aides assist the children to get out and go home? If all the adults are out there doing something different, what do you imagine the children and their families will think? They're going to start looking differently at the teachers. I mean, little things can make such a big difference.

Dr. Ackerman started the School Advisory Council because it was a way to get everybody at the table, working together. To me, everything starts with a conversation. Start a conversation with a parent, grandparent, or caring adult in your school. We may disagree, but guess what? We're sitting down having a conversation. We are both going to feel better when we leave that table, because we are going to be like, "Wow. I learned something. I thought we didn't share the same values, but I didn't understand that's what they were saying." And from that insight, system change, can happen.

Chapter 9
"Black and White Nomads—No Matter Where, We're Sticking Together, We Riding."

Looking back, I really think sometimes people in power do a disservice to poor people.

I've learned the school system is built in ways to hurt people that's poor. Why do middle-class, white people have to be in Black schools for the schools to become successful? Or, for people to start putting resources in the schools? Middle class Black people ain't putting resources in all Black public schools either, by the way. So, I don't even think it's about race anymore. I don't think in terms of white or Black people. I just say middle class people. Because, we have white and Black middle-class people who act like they're for us, but they don't want our poor children going to school with their children. They feel entitled, privileged to something better. It seems to me that folks that are poor and "don't know what they don't know" get nothing from schools.

When middle class parents advocate, people who run institutions respond to them. That's not necessarily the case for poor parents, whether African American or Latino. When they advocate there's a sense, "Well we can ride out their anger. They'll get tired and go away. And then we'll just keep going forward." They think, "What can they do to us?" And my thing is, these parents are advocating, they're fighting. Do I have to hit you in the head with a brick to see that they have rights?

I'm being honest. I feel as though I have played nice in the sandbox long enough. I'm angry now. I don't want to be angry 'cause I'm not an angry person. But I think that I'm at the point where I'm tired of being nice. I'm tired of going along to get along. The gloves are off. It's time to fight, 'cause we want the same things that everybody else wants. We are entitled to it. It's like, what makes you think that we shouldn't have the best of the best in our neighborhood because we're poor? What makes you think that we don't care because we're poor? What makes you think that we want our children and our grandchildren, to live the same way we live? Again, I think people think, "Oh, they'll get tired." We ain't getting tired. Yeah, we're tired but like Fannie Lou Hamer said, "We're sick and tired of being sick and tired." It's time to hold folks accountable, to make sure they do what they have to do. That's where I'm at now. I think this is that next door that's getting ready to open for me.

I don't want to be labeled as an angry Black person, but I see why Black, Latino, Asian, poor parents are angry. When I think of organizers who are trying to get poor white and Black people together, I think they just get them together to get them *together* on things. They're not trying to help these people become better citizens, become better parents, become better people. They are trying to make middle class people more powerful. I think of these non-profit and educational leaders as coming together to fight for a cause that's going to benefit the organizers, help them keep their own jobs!

If the system's working for you, then you're not interested in change. You're interested in just keeping it going because "it is working for me." So, when I was a commissioner, even though the system, for Sylvia P. Simms, was working, I knew it wasn't working for so many of my families. I was still getting phone calls from parents, still trying to open doors to all the families. How many other commissioners and educational leaders were doing the same thing? They don't want to see that reality of systemic failure and exclusion because that means more work. So I think there's a lot of people in this world who don't really want to see the truth. They want to put blinders on, but they're always willing to point the finger at what somebody else is doing. They always want to say that what you are doing is wrong or tell you what you are not doing right. But when do they look at themselves? Do they ask what can I do better? Or what have I done to make change? When I think of me being an organizer, I'm trying to get others to wake up so they can help the actual community.

That's why the work some organizers do, to me, is bullshit. I'm a community builder around education but at the end of the day, I'm trying to help a community of people.

I remember being at the public meeting about universal enrollment[23]. I wasn't a commissioner when this issue came up. I was still learning. I probably didn't understand exactly what was going on at the public meeting on this issue, but when I looked at those attending, there weren't a lot of people who looked like me, in that room. Who did the organizers think they were asking to come to this room? Why weren't there a lot of low-income families, whether it be Black, white, Latino, or Asian? I think these families weren't there because the district didn't want them in the room. They informed the people already in those magnet schools. "Come to this meeting." It wasn't told to people in poor neighborhoods. The district just wanted to hear from those parents who were saying "No, no, no, no, no universal enrollment."

But any time I see a lot of middle-class people fighting for or against something, it opens my eyes. It led me to ask, "Why are they against universal enrollment?" Why were none of the children from our communities going to the magnet schools?" And I was like, well there are a lot of reasons for that, but one of them shouldn't be because parents don't know there are such options. We should have people able to universally enroll across charter and regular public schools. Share the information and access. But people resisted. They thought they would lose something. I really never thought if somebody was to help me, that it would take away from them. I don't think life is like that. What I have, I have. It's for me. If I help somebody else, or if I share something else, that's not going to take away from what I have. It may grow more. I've never thought that if I help somebody, then that's taking away from me.

Here's another example: When I was commissioner, we needed to move teachers around in the schools. I said, if we're going to make change, we need to do it so we're not hurting people, folks still need to have a job. At the end of the day, people will say I'm against the unions. I am not against unions, I'm

93

against bad behavior. Listen, if you're not working and doing your job, you don't need your job. I don't care if I'm your union rep or not. You didn't do what you're supposed to do? Bye. So I told the teachers, "We still want you to have your job, but guess what? You're not going to be at Masterman[7]. You're going to be at Strawberry Mansion[8]. If you're a good teacher, and you're there for the children, why does it matter where you are?" When I said this idea publicly, people looked at me like I was crazy. They just kept the conversation moving. One of the other commissioners could have said, "Damn. Let's just try it. Even if we don't do the whole system, let's just do a network. Let's just see what happens in this network." But people were afraid to do stuff. Nobody said, "Hey, Sylvia. That's a good idea" Not one. If the other commissioners, even if two would have said it, it would have been passed. If two would have said "We'll play. We're going with that." But see? That's what I'm saying.

I once said something to the Mayor about only needing three votes to produce change. He said it don't work like that. There needed to be consensus. That only needing three was the "Street Sylvia" talking. That was the street. One, two, three, I'm gonna change this whole thing. And I probably would have been more of a pain in the butt than what I was being, because sometimes I was a pain in the butt, if I would have not gone for consensus, just gone for three. I really believe that there was a lot of people that didn't want me at that table, because being at that table showed them how they weren't really doing what they thought they were. I was a reminder that this isn't working. Cause you see, where is the me that's sitting on the school board now? Who's the Sylvia that is sitting on the school board? I know my people. I know what my people need. I know what they want. And a lot of times people didn't want to hear that. Because if you're the superintendent, or you're the people that's making the decisions, you don't want to hear things are going wrong. You want to hear, "Oh! The schools are great." "Oh, the children

---

7   Julia R. Masterman Laboratory and Demonstration School in the Spring Garden neighborhood of Philadelphia. Masterman is a magnet school ranked 10th in the United States

8   Strawberry Mansion High School, a public high school in the Strawberry Mansion neighborhood of Philadelphia

are learning." But, no. You are lying. Children are not learning. I always say there's so many games being played on the backs of our children. And when are we going to say enough is enough?

But change is hard. I think I shared this earlier when I was talking about how all these Black parents got together and went to Washington, D.C. for the National Elementary Secondary Education Advisory Coalition. Now, these were parents from the poorest communities in the United States. I tell you, we're in the house. I was just like, "Wow." And I was right there. I was representing. *PARENT POWER* was representing. We were tired of our children not being educated. "We're tired of our schools failing our children." It was a very, very big movement. But we weren't really organized. It was just a whole bunch of Black parents wanting to make change. We didn't do our due diligence, as an organization, to come together. We were just some Black, angry parents in Washington, D.C., acting crazy. So you know what they did? They shut that organization down. We weren't organized to stop them, to make change.

And here's why: Like I said before, we don't have time to organize. I think white middle-class parents, they have the time. They're able to do things that we can't do. So even though there is more of us than there is them, it's so hard because we lack the time. When you're unemployed, you can't spend all your time organizing. I mean it was one thing when this was my job, and I had time to do this because this was my job. But it's hard. And it's even harder when you know deep in your heart that you just can't get to it because you have to support yourself, your family. I have some parent leaders who are with me, but because I'm going through my own trials and tribulations, I'm trying to focus on me right now. And that really hurts me. It does. It really hurts me. I'm there for them, but I can't be there for them the way I want to be. It hurts me. I try to talk to my parent leaders all of the time, because that's all I can give them is love. I can still do the workshops, I can still do the trainings, but right now, I'm not there to help with their children being bullied, thrown out of school. It hurts. I could talk to you three days, and you still don't understand what I'm talking about, but ...

I've learned so much because, like I said, I am the families that I serve. And now I'm tired of being nice.

So, Lori, you and I, we're gonna start a movement. There used to be a motorcycle club called the Black and white Nomads. I always loved that name, even when I was a little girl, "Black and white Nomads, no matter what, we're sticking together, we're riding." I don't know if that's what the group meant, but what I mean is, "You're white. I'm Black. We're poor." Next time we meet, you bring your white friends. I'll bring my Black friends. We'll keep going forward. I think this is how things change - having those crucial conversations. We don't have to ask permission. If there's something that people want to do, we just do it. Who can stop us? I think a lot of things don't happen because of fear. Or people don't have the conversation needed to make it happen. People keep pitting people against each other, because the person who believes "B" ain't going with the people who believe "A" to come together. So, their job, their vision and mission, to keep us from having conversations, because they know we ain't in agreement. We Black or we white. But I think if you're kind and you're caring, you can connect to people. It cuts across how people are dressed, cuts across what group they're in. You can get to the human side of them and you can connect. I mean if a poor, Black woman can meet with the poor white women, maybe we can get some crucial conversations going. Maybe we can create some systemic change to help the poor. I don't know, but I would love to give it a try.

It's time for the Black and White Nomads to get busy.

It's about PARENT POWER for the poor.

What will you do with yours?

ENDNOTES

1. Increased accountability for schools, school districts, and states.

2. Parent Leadership Academy was a pilot effort of the School District of Philadelphia and the William Penn Foundation to empower and promote the development of parents as leaders in their children's education and schools. PLA was designed as a joint initiative of parents and the District. During its time of operation, between 2005 and 2008, PLA was able to provide valuable programs to over 1,000 parents.

3. Family Leadership Institute is a multi-session, in-depth training for families to build knowledge and leadership skills related to special education and health care sponsored at no cost to families by the PEAL Center, the Medical Home Initiative, Research for Human Development & Philadelphia Department of Health, Division of Child & Family Health.

4. Arlene Ackerman was the Philadelphia Public Schools Superintendent from May 2008 to November 2011

5. National Coalition of ESEA Title 1 Parents Conference is aimed at coordinating among different federal education programs under the Elementary and Secondary Education Act (ESEA).

6. Paul Valles was CEO of Philadelphia Public School July 2002 – June 2007

7. War on Poverty is the unofficial name that refers to legislation introduced by President Lyndon B. Johnson in his State of the Union address in 1964. He proposed sweeping legislation, including establishing Title I funding for schools and the Office of Economic Opportunity (OEO) to address a growing poverty rate in the United States.

8. Elementary, Secondary Education Act, also referred to as ESEA, was passed as part of President Lyndon Johnson's "War on Poverty". Title I under ESEA focuses on closing the skill gap in reading, writing, and mathematics for children from low-income households.

9. CASTOR Form refers to the Title 1 parent/guardian consent form

10. State Advisory Councils were established in the Head Start Act. They require the governor of each state to establish an advisory council on Early Childhood Education and Care for children from birth to school entry.

11. Shirley Kitchen was a member of the Pennsylvania Senate from the 3rd district (Pennsylvania's third congressional district includes several areas of the city of Philadelphia, including West Philadelphia, most of Center City, and parts of North Philadelphia). She was in office November 18, 1996 to November 30, 2016.

12. Community Innovation Zone Grant is a Pennsylvania Department of Education grant awarded to expand local programs that help bridge the achievement gap for at-risk young children.

13. Turnaround schools involve short-term interventions taken by the state or district to dramatically improve an underperforming school. Charter schools are schools that receive public funding but operate separately from the public school district through establishment of a school charter and governing body. Traditional Public schools are publicly funded and open to all students. Mastery and KIPP schools refer to two charter organizations. Mastery operates 24 schools in Philadelphia and Camden, NJ, while KIPP operates 275 schools throughout the United States. Catholic schools are educational institutions operated in association with the Catholic Church.

14. Superintendent Bill Hite was Superintendent of the Philadelphia School District from 2012-2022.

15. Title 1 Parent Advisory Council was created by the Pennsylvania Department of Education to involve parents of Title I students in sharing ideas with the Division of Federal Programs to help increase student achievement.

16. Pedro Ramos has been President and CEO of the Philadelphia Foundation since 2015

17. School Reform Commission is the governing body for the school district of Philadelphia. With five members appointed by the Governor and Mayor, they are responsible for making decisions in the best interests of all the students in the district.

18. School Advisory Councils in Philadelphia are peer-elected, collaborative teams composed of families, the school principal, teachers and other school-based staff, students, and community members. The council focuses on having data-driven conversations to help improve school achievement and effective teaching.

19. Promise Academies were an initiative started in 2010 in the Philadelphia School District. It involved pouring additional money into under-resourced and low-performing schools and was spearheaded by Arlene Ackerman while she was serving as the superintendent. The initiative was ultimately unsuccessful due to issues with funding, leadership, and teacher layoffs.

20. Mastery Charter is a charter school network based in Philadelphia and Camden, NJ. They currently run 24 schools and have taken over several failing Philadelphia Public Schools, including Simon Gratz High School.

21. Read by 4th program is an early literacy initiative in the city of Philadelphia, which provides support to families and schools to increase rates of early literacy in children from low-income neighborhoods.

22. Neighborhood Advisory Committees are organizations that help residents learn about programs in the city of Philadelphia that could benefit them, including reducing homelessness, reducing energy costs, developing resident job skills, and mentoring youth.

23. Universal Enrollment is a model of school enrollment in which parents/families would submit one application for schools. The model allows families to rank their school choices and streamlines the enrollment process.

Author and Editor Profiles

Sylvia P. Simms, of Philadelphia, is an advocate for high-quality education – especially in low-income neighborhoods. Simms is the founder of PARENT POWER, a training program to get families more involved in their children's education and has been involved with community improvement efforts for more than a decade. She also works for SELF Inc. as a Housing Support Coach. SELF Inc. is a human services agency that provides emergency and permanent supportive housing, housing-focused case management, mentoring, and other vital services and resources for Philadelphia's most vulnerable communities.

Dr. Lori Shorr earned her doctoral degree in Critical and Cultural studies with an emphasis on how social changes are connected to, and influenced by, narratives - be they political, historical, social or personal. She has culminated a 20-year career in policy development and implementation from Special Assistant to three Pennsylvania Secretaries of Education to eight years as the Chief Education Officer for the City of Philadelphia, which entailed setting the mayor's policy agenda in K-12 and higher education. The courses she teaches and the work she continues to do in the community, as well as the mentoring she does with students, is therefore centered around the theories which help to explain how power, representation, constructions of social justice and community interact with the "lived experiences" and policy realities in specific historical junctions.

www.ingramcontent.com/pod-product-compliance
Lightning Source LLC
Chambersburg PA
CBHW041720090426
42739CB00019B/3491